"*This is a tremendously useful book by one of Canada's best broadcasters.*"
Peter Herrndorf, Director General, National Arts Centre

"*Finally, a highly readable book about good Canadian English, rooted ... in sound grammar and usage. Bruce's sharp wit and broadcasting experience make this book a 'must have' for anyone who gives a damn about Canadian English.*"
Russ Germaine, "The World at Six," CBC Radio National News

"*This book is professional, comprehensive, fun, and tremendously helpful for anyone with a fear of presenting themselves in public. Designed for the media professional,* You Can Say That Again *is just as helpful for any business executive who has to make speeches, reports, presentations, or simply approach the boss for a raise.... Surveys show business executives fear presentations and speeches with a passion. Bruce replaces the fear with a good dose of confidence.*"
Barrie Doyle, President, Gateway Communications, Instructor, Humber College

"You Can Say That Again *is the new guide for my students, for the profession, for those with an interest in the world's languages, and (with the trivia quiz in each chapter) for those who love word games.*"
Jon Keeble, Chairman, Radio and Television Arts, Ryerson Polytechnical University

"*I prefer to associate with those who believe pronouncing words correctly is not only satisfying ... but fun! So does Bruce Rogers who has long set the standard for Canadians who enjoy using the English language properly....*"
Peter Kent, Global Television News

You Can Say That Again!

You Can Say That Again!

A Fun Approach to Sounding Better When You Open Your Mouth to Speak

Bruce Rogers

HOUNSLOW PRESS
A MEMBER OF THE DUNDURN GROUP
TORONTO · OXFORD

Hounslow Press
A Member of the Dundurn Group

Publisher: Anthony Hawke
Editor: Liedewy Hawke
Design: Jennifer Scott
Printer: Webcom

Canadian Cataloguing in Publication Data

Rogers, Bruce (Bruce A.)
You Can Say That Again:
a fun approach to sounding better when you open your mouth to speak

Includes bibliographical references and index.
ISBN 0-88882-208-1

1. Public speaking. I. Title

PN4121.R63 1999   808.5"1   C99-931993-0

1   2   3   4   5   03   02   01   00   99

We acknowledge the support of the **Canada Council for the Arts** for our publishing program. We also acknowledge the support of the **Ontario Arts Council**. We acknowledge the financial support of the Government of Canada through the Book Publishing Industry Development Program (BPIDP) for our publishing activities.

Care has been taken to trace the ownership of copyright material used in this book. The author and the publisher welcome any information enabling them to rectify any references or credit in subsequent editions.

J. Kirk Howard, President

Printed and bound in Canada.

Printed on recycled paper.

Dundurn Press	Dundurn Press	Dundurn Press
8 Market Street	73 Lime Walk	2250 Military Road
Suite 200	Headington, Oxford,	Tonawanda, New York
Toronto, Ontario, Canada	England	U.S.A. 14150
M5E 1M6	OX3 7AD	

To Diana

TABLE OF CONTENTS

Words are power • Standards matter • Good speech: "Cultivated formal," mid-Atlantic • The use of *youse* • "Japanglish" • Ebonics • The democratic populist versus the pedantic snob

Formal and informal speech • Canadian English • Phonetic systems • Accent and intonation • Vocal presentation: tips on phrasing, breathing, emphasis • Some terms and symbols

Theories about the origins of speech • Tracking our Indo-European language roots • Grimm's Law • The Tower of Babel • Phoenician — our alphabet • Linggwistik Reformation • Semantics

Etymology — a list of words and their history, from *abracadabra* to *zythepsary* • Slang and jargon • Spoonerisms and euphemisms • Puns and limericks • Bowdlerizing • Swearing • What does - *30* - mean?

list of business terms • Clichés • Confusing headlines • A few words of advice

A balanced approach to good speech

Phonetic guides • Tips on pronunciation for major world languages including Arabic, Chinese, Danish, French, German, Italian, Norwegian, Portuguese, Russian, Spanish, Swedish, and others • Language protectionism • Quebec French • Goldilocks in Italian • A Yiddish Night before Chanukah

Forewords

Years ago, in a CBC radio studio on the seventh floor of the Château Laurier in Ottawa, two young and relatively new announcers launched a program called "Carte Blanche."

Bruce Rogers and I felt we were breaking new ground with a show that would push the envelope by mixing music and commentary in a friendly way. While the presentation was very informal, it had to adhere to the strict broadcast standards drilled into us during our early CBC years. The language had to be clear and precise and totally free of solecisms. There was, of course, no tolerance for wrong information and we were expected to pay attention to the protocol of an earlier broadcasting age. We were regarded as invited guests in listeners' homes and had to behave accordingly. Our little project was judged a success, and while we had great fun doing it, we learned something important. Both of us came away from the exercise with the clear understanding that you could pay attention to language and good presentation and still be an effective communicator.

Bruce went on to become a highly succesful host and broadcast journalist in both public and private sectors. When we met over the years we often deplored the slippage in the standards we continued to honour. We understood that the climate had changed and presentations had to be more relaxed but felt there was no excuse for some of the sloppiness and lack of respect for language that has become all too prevalent on our nation's airwaves. Too often, a glaring mispronunciation or an outrageous mistake in grammar can mar a great effort.

With this book Bruce steps foward to fill a need. It's an entertaining approach that is also a serious attempt to arrest the drift away from any kind of moderately acceptable standard for the spoken word. This book is not pedantic and doesn't preach a cure. *You Can Say That Again* is timely and amusing and useful for anyone ... broadcaster or after-dinner speaker ... who wants to make a good impression.

LLOYD ROBERTSON
CTV News

After three and a half decades as a broadcast journalist — perhaps a third of that time at an anchor desk of one sort or another — I'm all too familiar with the mortifying agony of mispronunciation as well as the exhilarating, self-satisfied high triggered by the successful negotiation of a word minefield.

I still occasionally find myself fighting the wave of panic that can be generated by unexpected confrontation with a potentially disastrous assembly of vowels, consonants, and syllables.

It's easy to laugh today about the simply sloppy pronunciations. As a matter of fact, in my early, highly unprofessional days in private radio, I have to admit I occasionally laughed at myself, while still on the air. The example I remember best: "... the huge crowd that 'messed' in a Buenos Aires square"!

In ten years working for the American television network NBC I agonized over the pronunciation of *been* (they say **BIN**), *semi* (they split between **SEM-ee** and **SEM-eye**), not to mention our notorious *out* and *about*.

But you have to be a broadcaster to squirm after being tripped up by the pronunciation of a local or foreign landmark. Balliol Avenue (in Toronto) got me when I first arrived in Toronto from Calgary (Torontonians say **BELL-OIL** as opposed to the British **BELL-ee-ALL**). And I still blush at the memory of the time I asked a London cabbie to take me to Beauchamp Place. Anyone familiar with the Knightsbridge district just knows the British pronounce the street name as though it were spelled Beecham!!

When it comes to correct pronunciation, I fall somewhere between the painfully — sometimes pompously — fastidious and those who associate proper usage with snobs and poseurs.

In the end, I think I prefer to associate with those who believe that pronouncing words correctly is not only satisfying — but fun.

So, I believe, does Bruce Rogers, an individual who has long set the standard for Canadians who enjoy using the English language properly for work and pleasure.

PETER KENT
Global Television News

Acknowledgements

A labour of love like this book is a time-consuming preoccupation. My wife, Diana, was understanding and tolerant of the concentration it took to research and write it.

Others were encouraging too, including wordmeister, broadcaster, and writer Jeremy Brown. Some colleagues took a real interest and encouraged me to press on: "Remind readers there's no such word as irregardless." "Tell them it's pronounced Or-jee!" "How about a note on kilometre?"

My most influential mentor was always consulting the dictionary, interested in Latin roots. My father's interest in words, language, and good speech was contagious. Harry "H. H." Rogers worked at building his vocabulary through his entire eighty-seven years and his love of words rubbed off on me. More important than that, he read me *Uncle Wiggly*, *Pinocchio*, and *Black Beauty* when I was small.

Another prime and wordy influence was the late E. U. "Ted" Schrader, newspaperman and chairman of the Journalism School at Ryerson in the early sixties. While serious about correct and simple English, he encouraged fun with words. Also on the Ryerson faculty then, and determined to instill a love of language and good speech, was Jim Peters. His invaluable phonetic guide is listed in the bibliography.

At CBC, the guardian of language, the late W. H. Brodie, emphasized clarity and understanding. He insisted on correct pronunciation but simple and natural expression. No pedantry allowed. Other important influences during my years at CBC included Angus McLellan and Bert Cowan of National Radio News. Conscientious colleagues at CFRB News influenced me too, in the late fifties and again in the nineties.

Other influential colleagues who set a high standard included Harry Mannis, Lamont Tilden, Ken Haslam, Frank Herbert, John Envers, John

O'Leary, Harry Brown, Bill Paul, Bruce Marsh, Jim Chorley, John Rae, Alan McFee, Lloyd Robertson, and Bernard "Bunny" Cowan. Unfortunately I can't list all of the professional and influential confreres who worked in that collegial environment during what we all agree were "the best days" at old "Mother Corp."

At TVO, punster, linguist, and my "old china plate" Dr. Rob Buckman has encouraged me with his tips on Cockney slang and his wild sense of humour. He knows his words and has shared his delight with me.

Others helpful in getting this tome into print were Tony Hawke and Liedewy Hawke of Dundurn Press. Thanks to all of the above. Whether it was a word to check, their influence over the years, or other contributions — I'm grateful. But any errors of fact or opinion are entirely mine.

*Start your day by brushing your teeth
and sharpening your tongue!*
— Oscar Levant

INTRODUCTION

Words Are Power

Mend your speech a little lest it may mar your fortune.
— Shakespeare

You say "tomato" (tuh-MAY-toe). I say "tum-AH-toe." Ditto for potato. So, as the song proposes, should we "call the whole thing off"? Hardly. Some pronunciation differences just make things interesting. Pronunciation errors, however, can also erode our credibility. Or, to put it positively, credible speech is power. Correct pronunciation confers authority and builds confidence. If we make our point clearly and naturally, our verbal assurance grows.

Feel free to sound out the words and move your lips as you read this book. You may chuckle or crack a smile as you play with words and check how to say them. At the very least, you'll have some word trivia fun.

One use for this book is as a handy, preliminary reference; something to check before going to the dictionary or specialized pronunciation guides. It also tries to settle an argument within myself. On the one hand I'm often disappointed, sometimes annoyed, when I hear broadcasters kick the language around with poor speech, poor grammar, and incorrect pronunciation. On the other hand, I almost always side with those who argue for flexibility while reminding us that English is constantly changing. Meanings change. Pronunciation evolves. The argument simmers through this book, ending in an uneasy truce, the dispute unresolved.

The book tries to foster greater affection for language and its proper use. And it may lead to greater vocal comfort and help avoid embarrassment. For instance, it helps to know that a cohort is not an associate but a group of Roman soldiers. It helps to know *engine* is pronounced "**EN-jin**," not "**IN-jun**."

It may even be handy to know when to use the word *ferkin* and how it differs from *merkin*. These are not the names of a vaudeville act like Frick and Frack. Check Chapter 5 for their meanings.

Journalists who entertain and inform should be rated on those two criteria. They should not be harshly judged for occasional lapses in the use of *who* versus *whom* or for occasional split infinitives or dangling participles. But frequent abuse of the language is another matter, especially if it's in the broadcast media. And the offence is even greater if it's heard on CBC.

There are those who appear to pride themselves on making up their own rules like Humpty Dumpty in *Alice in Wonderland.* Their carelessness or ignorance can be amusing, as was this headline written by some inattentive editor:

NEW STUDY OF OBESITY LOOKS FOR LARGER TEST GROUP

But often we lose all respect for the person who has displayed either ignorance or a cavalier attitude.

STANDARDS MATTER

Standards of speech and grammar have plummeted in recent years. Television, advertising, radio, and films are major contributors to the decline. It's not just a matter of the constant, healthy evolution of language. And it isn't simply an infusion of non-standard varieties of English in a multicultural society.

Educators may be partly responsible for the deterioration. But they struggle against a tide of linguistic barbarism. The environment in which they teach is fouled by the communications priorities of commerce and by the popular trivialization of media content.

Post-secondary educators complain that many of their students, both undergraduate and graduate, are unable to write grammatical sentences or a well-reasoned argument. In the groves of academe few students pick the fruit from the highest branches. Most are content to take a shortcut through the orchard on the way to an entry-level job. And colleges as well as universities seem to be ready to assist those students who wish to avoid scholarship. Curriculum 101 provides a bare introduction to history, English literature, political science, or whatever. Students are able to choose one subject from column A and one from column B — a Chinese-menu course of studies. As a result, when they graduate, many of them are ill-equipped. Their language skills are inferior.

It is true that language is not static. The way we express ourselves is influenced by technology, the economy, immigration, politics, fashion, demographics, and many other factors. 'Twas ever thus. And with each stage of language development there has been resistance to change and heavy criticism of new modes of expression. After consistent spelling became widespread, deviation was seen as the start of a slide down a slippery slope. Spelling and pronunciation changes were even seen as issues of morality. At the very least, language nonconformists were seen as less than respectable. Schoolchildren who used non-standard English were stereotyped and marked for academic failure. If they spoke Caribbean, Asian, or African English they were stigmatized. Fortunately there is wider recognition today that one's language variety, accent, dialect, and even vocabulary are closely linked to one's identity and self-respect. This is not a plea for acceptance of Ebonics or street slang. It is still an advantage to use the language that prevails in higher education and in international communication even while we are more tolerant of other varieties of English.

To return to the core problem, we enjoy huge leaps in communications technology but our ability to connect with one another declines. The language of the popular media is a vernacular of limited scope. It has potent emotional range but is intellectually stunted. Privileged people find the information they need whatever the source, from narrow-interest technical journals to Web sites. But the mass audience is served predigested, oversimplified pap in language designed to eliminate thought. It's a new illiteracy. And it undermines the assumption that a democratic society should be based on a widely shared understanding of what's going on.

Advertisers target children and adolescents of limited language development. Not a problem perhaps, even when they use low-brow language. Except, the special language becomes the norm. For example, children don't learn the useful distinction between an adverb and an adjective. So we hear expressions like, "Drive safe!" and, "Lose weight quick!" No big deal? Maybe it's just language in evolution again. But the problem is greater than this minor example of usage change. Peer pressure confirms incorrect but popular usage.

We know that young children only gradually come to understand and use the tools of grammar. Matters of agreement, or of plural and singular, come into use only as a result of maturation and education. Until then, the words *she* and *her* may be interchangeable. "He coming," is likely. So are double, even triple negatives. The same goes for vocabulary development and pronunciation.

Television and radio cater to that level of language development in order to keep their audience and so that advertisers will buy time. This turns into a general problem when the young audience becomes the prime target and when those standards begin to dominate the popular media, including news and public affairs.

But when the targets of filmmakers and the tabloids also possess limited language skills, these poor habits of speech become the common denominator and the standard. Then it's an uphill struggle for teachers, parents, conscientious broadcasters, and writers. In fact, those who encourage more sophisticated language use are sometimes called elitist and undemocratic.

You Can Say That Again!

Thank heavens for some of the newspapers. The middle-class broadsheets still have editors and still acknowledge their responsibility to contribute to literate discourse. While more of their content is gossip these days, they still try to avoid oversimplification. They demand of their reporters, columnists, and news writers some degree of literacy. They serve a readership that enjoys a rich range of expression and expects conformity to established standards of usage. The tabloids, on the other hand, are designed for the marginally literate, those who like lots of pictures, simple words, and big print; those whose lips move when they read. The tabloids keep it simple. They don't confuse the reader with the complexity of facts and the ambiguity of the human condition. They keep the issues black or white, right or wrong, win or lose. That doesn't require much of a vocabulary or any subtlety of expression. And that approach applies to most television, popular radio, and most advertising.

So this book is partly a reaction to a contemporary dumbing-down and carelessness that threatens the quality of public discourse. It is for the individual who wants to communicate well without drawing attention to his or her manner of speech. The decline of recent years undermines our ability to communicate effectively or with subtlety about the complexities and nuances of social issues. We share less and less. And many individuals, accomplished in other ways, find their lives and careers circumscribed by the limitations of their language.

Take pronunciation for example. Broadcasters who should know better say *schism* as **SKIZ-um** instead of the correct **SIZ-um**. (Now there's dispute about this. **SIZ-um** is no longer preferred in some quarters. See Chapter 5, Words.) Others say **kil-AWM-it-ir** instead of **KIL-o-meet-ir**. *Flaccid* is correctly **FLAK-sid**, not **FLAS-id**. *Accede* is **AK-seed**, not **a-SEED**! Mistakes as common as these are heard all too often from TV anchors, radio hosts, and after-dinner speakers. Some years ago a CBC TV news anchor called the Jewish holiday **chan-OO-ka** (Chanukah). More recently a 680 News anchor referred to the Irish Republican Army's political wing Sinn Fein (**SHIN FAIN**) as **SIN FINE** (to rhyme with *shine* instead of *rain*). This book encourages a slightly higher standard, but chances are we'll win some and lose some.

This is not just another case of one generation resisting the vocal expression of a younger one. Nor is it geezerhood versus the nonconformity of youth. But it is a somewhat curmudgeonly attempt to maintain the richness and elegance of our communication efforts. This book is written out of respect for the greatest of human achievements — our language.

If it helps some individuals to a higher standard of usage in the media and on the public platform, so much the better. If those who read it also enjoy themselves, that's a great reward. At least, it may foment some healthy, language-focused debate.

Introduction

Knowing more words makes us smarter. A broad vocabulary combined with an understanding of the rules of good usage helps us read more quickly, understand more readily, and retain more of what we read. And better use of words impresses others and confers power. That puts us in a position to take advantage of opportunities. With words, as in so many other ways, nothing succeeds like success. While the rewards of self improvement, greater social confidence, and a career boost are laudable goals, the book's primary purpose is to be an everyday aid to better English usage.

There is, however, no language expert to serve as arbiter in all disputes about usage, spelling, grammar, and pronunciation. And this book won't fill that void.

A love of words probably begins in infancy. Parents who love words instill that love in their children. Those children enjoy a significant advantage. Children who are read bedtime stories soon develop an interest in reading for themselves. They start school with a bigger vocabulary and an advanced ability to learn. Some teachers have a knack for encouraging children. A love of words and language is soon conveyed to students. The communication tool kit of the early school years becomes the foundation for scholarship and personal growth. Affectation and pedantry aren't necessary. In fact, they can kill curiosity. All that's necessary is a shared love of words.

There is little patience in these pages for "reactionary nostalgia" as the *Guide to Canadian English Usage* by Margery Fee and Janice McAlpine (1997) puts it. Some people like to confront each departure from the "rules." This book will disappoint those hobbyists.

The use of language as a moral yardstick goes back to the eighteenth century, when English was being standardized in dictionaries. There were references then to the "vulgar" language of the "common people." But language isn't a simple matter of right and wrong. It is simply that you are more likely to be persuasive when you follow convention than when you flout it. "Like, uh, yuh know, me and him ain't got no tickets, eh? So, uh, like, we can't go wid youse," may be commonly heard but it doesn't leave a good impression or connect effectively. You are more likely to be found credible and more likely to be understood if you stick with standard educated usage in spelling, grammar, and pronunciation.

Keeping up with constant change is difficult. What's acceptable today may be unacceptable tomorrow. Sometimes there is a Canadian pronunciation. In these pages that is usually preferred. Emphasis on the prefix in *repeat* is American, **ruh-PEET** is Canadian. But in Canada, depending on location and occasion, you may have a choice among the favoured Canadian, American, and British pronunciations. Lots of

Canadians say *coyote* "**KY-yoot**," but many have seen a lot of film and TV westerns, so they say "**ky-OH-tee**." The NHL team gets the American pronunciation (**ky-OH-tee**) from most sportscasters. Is it another word undergoing Americanization?

GOOD SPEECH: CULTIVATED FORMAL

Standard English is a convenient abstraction like the average man.
— G. L. Brook

The section on English phonetic values assumes North American, largely Canadian, sometimes called "mid-Atlantic" values, clearly influenced by the best speech of educated Londoners and having a lot in common with the good speech of Toronto or New York. The word *research* is variously pronounced depending on where you are and how your parents spoke. Americans tend to emphasize prefixes, so *research* is pronounced **REE-surch**. The Oxford dictionary prefers the emphasis on the second syllable (**ruh-SURCH**), and that's the preferred pronunciation in Canada as well as in Britain. "Cultivated formal" is the standard in this book, but a common, everyday vernacular is also acknowledged.

In these pages the nitpicking reader may find provocative usage and pronunciation, intentional in some instances but undetected by author or editor in others. Preference for one way rather than another may be simply a matter of opinion. What one has always heard may be comfortable but not necessarily correct (**ASH-fawlt** for *asphalt*). On the other hand, what was recorded in a past dictionary or what is preferred in some ivory tower may be unfamiliar in popular speech. This book is full of judgement calls but it won't settle all arguments.

Like salted peanuts, words and language are addictive. This book touches on phonetics, word origins, spoonerisms, and jargon. But it is not a pronouncing dictionary. It simply pulls together word-wisdom from a variety of sources.

Good speech is essential equipment, a matter of good manners. It is necessary for easy, polite authority and leadership. While this is not a "greater influence through word power" kind of book, it argues that good speech commands attention (at the office, socially, and on the podium). Words are power.

Your knowledge of words may be your most important skill. It is valuable to be computer competent and to have at least rudimentary mathematical ability, even though calculators and computers do much of the "donkey work" today. But an ability to communicate effectively is indispensable. A spell check might help, but when it comes to using the appropriate word and saying it so others will understand, you are on your own. An example of misunderstanding from the time of the forced exodus from Newfoundland's outports is the answer an elderly woman gave when a doctor examined her. "Have you ever been bedridden?" he asked. "Yus," she answered proudly, "and once in a dory!"

IT'S SHOE TIME!

A malapropism can provide a laugh. Examples abound in sports and politics. You'll find some in this book. But there can be a real cost attached. For instance, Nike's TV spot in which Samburu tribesmen in Kenya say the Nike slogan in Maa, their native tongue. The trouble is, a watchful American anthropologist knows the language and reveals that a tribesman is really saying, "I don't want these. Give me big shoes." Nike also recalled thirty-eight thousand pairs of shoes with a logo that offended Muslims. The logo resembled the Arabic word *Allah,* the Muslim name for God. Since shoes get dirty, it was thought to be disrespectful. After the apology and withdrawal, Muslim authorities agreed not to ask for a boycott of Nike shoes.

Then there was Reebok's goof when it named a shoe after a Greek mythological character, Incubus. Trouble is, the ancient demon was notorious for raping women while they slept. Good for the image? Hardly! How about Coca-Cola's pitch in China? It said when translated, "Bite the wax tadpole!" Or the new Ford introduced in Latin America, the *Fiera,* which means "ugly, old woman" in Spanish. By the way, the cola slogan, "It's the real thing!" was the term used by Blackfoot people for the meat of the plains bison or buffalo. They called it *nitapiksisako.*

PRONUNCIATION

Without knowing the force of words, it is impossible to know men.
— Confucius

This guide offers an easy introduction to phonetics with a simple, layman's system. Along with language trivia, word origins, and a guide to how to say many commonly mispronounced words in English, the book includes hints on major foreign languages (see Appendix B). It deals with presentation issues, including speech skills, valuable for social and career success.

What is a *petard*? What are *ehryn*? How do you say *asphalt* and *schism*? What about *larynx*?[1]

The answers are in this book. It is crucial to know what words mean and how to use them in a logical, persuasive manner. We all want to express our thoughts clearly and say the words correctly.

First impressions are critical. Along with our grooming, dress, and manners, our speech leaves an immediate, indelible impression. Others assess us on the basis of what they learn in those first few moments. That evaluation can influence further dealings either favourably or unfavourably.

On that first social transaction we judge another person's social skills, their intellectual capacity, and their leadership qualities. Poor speech leads to conclusions, whether that is fair or not. That's why good speech, including pronunciation, matters. Good writing and good speech leave a positive impression. They establish credibility and enhance authority.

In business and social situations, *how* you say it is often as important as *what* you say. The articulate, confident individual gets ahead. Those who speak well succeed.

We all want to build self esteem and gain respect. But the task involves more than just building vocabulary, even though that's a rewarding self-improvement project. A basic vocabulary (of six thousand words) used well may serve as effectively as a huge one, if it is used with precision and creativity. (Better to say *tireless* than *indefatigable*.) So, while this book might add a few words to one's vocabulary, its aim is to help the reader improve speech — to *sound* better.

If a waitress or waiter sets your teeth on edge with "What would youse like?" you understand how everyday speech leaves an impression, often a poor one. In fact, the form *youse* as a plural, a collective of *you*, is simply an archaic form, no longer in favour. Today it is regarded as poor usage.[2]

WORDS FOR SUCCESS

When we hear a name being mispronounced, we wince. If we hear a common term being mangled, we feel embarrassed for the speaker. Of course we can't know every specialized technical term in every vocation. So, when a term stumps us we ask or look it up. And that's a good habit. But too often we assume we know the correct meaning and pronunciation for words frequently seen in print. So we don't look them up. And, from time to time, we're caught with our smarts down. We want to avoid becoming pedantic, but we don't want to be thought ignorant either. That's why we make an effort to avoid errors in everyday speech.

We're all vulnerable. While a verbal miscue is often just an embarrassing moment — perhaps a temporary loss of credibility — sometimes the *faux pas* (**FO-paw**) can be career-threatening. A language goof is enough to destroy the hard-won credibility of a politician or journalist.

We don't have to become multilingual sophisticates, but we can have some fun and enlarge our comfort zone by learning certain basics about

Introduction

English and other major languages. We can have some fun and enjoy immediate rewards by adding a few new words to our everyday speech and using them correctly. Say it with confidence and gain authority.

WORDS ARE THOUGHT

Words are absolutely necessary for thinking, and with a minimum of words there is a minimum of thought.
— Aubrey A. Douglas

Words enable us to think. The greater our vocabulary, the more complex and subtle our thoughts. Concepts require words and an ease with the logic of language. It's a fact, people who are at ease with more words are smarter. And, like blondes, logophiles have more fun.

ENGLISH AND PHONETICS

We all like to sound as though we know what we are talking about. Therefore, this book focuses on how to use and say those English words that are so often misused or mispronounced. English is not a phonetic language like Spanish, French, or Italian. English breaks the rules. It's full of oddities. Some of the tricks take us back to the Jutes, the Angles, and Saxons. Others take us back to William the Conqueror. Some even whisk us back to the time of Hadrian or Caesar. In any case, the spelling doesn't always help.

- *Hearth* is pronounced **HARTH**, not **HEERTH** (as heard on a Toronto radio station).
- *Posthumously* is pronounced **PAWS-tyuh-mus-lee**, not **post-HYOO-mus-lee**.
- *Decorative* is **DEK-'ruh-tiv**, not **duh-KOR-uh-tiv** (as heard on TV).

These examples demonstrate both the issue of correct sounds, in instances when spelling might mislead us, and the problem of emphasis on the right syllable. This book begins with a look at pronunciation systems and tips on dividing words into syllables for easy emphasis.

WORD ORIGINS

An etymological list is an amusing way to consider language history. The ancient story of the Tower of Babel foretells the development of many languages from a single source. Does it also ask the more modern question whether we are programmed to develop language?

English traces its roots to eastern Europe, to sometime between 3000 and 500 B.C. It evolved with heavy influences from Teutons, Romans, Anglo-Saxons, Vikings, and the Norman French. Then came the printing press and the long, slow trend to spelling conformity. Later still, exploration, colonialism, and modern communication technology had their impact. Radio, television, and the computer have all been major influences on vocabulary and the way we speak. The evolution of English is the best argument against artificial rigidity. English has picked up words from all over the world and has influenced languages everywhere. In Japan, people are fighting to preserve their language in the face of an attack of English or something akin to it. The Japanese health ministry has a problem with *raifu sapooto adobaizaa* (life support advisory). Neo-English turns up in words like *akauntabiriti* (accountability). Even TV ads use "Japanglish" like *creap* for coffee cream. While Japanese use a French word for bread, *pan*, the big foreign influence is American. Golf is *gorufu*. On the other hand, this book explores the many words we assume are English but which actually came to us from other languages.

WHICH ENGLISH?

Then there's the special English of the Cockney Londoner, a speech now quickly disappearing, and vanishing along with it is the street skill of rhyming slang. There are contending stories about the origin of the word *Cockney*: one is that the term comes from France, where visiting Londoners were identified at one time by the plumes or cockades on their hats. More on Cockney English later.

Yet another English is the controversial "Black English" of California and some other parts of the United States and Canada. *Ebonics* has entered the vocabulary along with some new syntax. There's also the English of the Caribbean. And the English of Newfoundland. There are many dialects and accents. For instance the "Strine" of Australia. Sometimes two English speakers from different parts of the globe, or even from two different urban neighbourhoods, have difficulty understanding one another.

In these pages, slang, jargon, and euphemisms get the slighting attention they deserve; they are not ignored, just *belittled* (an American colonial word used by Jefferson and ridiculed by the gentry back in King George III's England). There is also a small collection of words and terms from the world of politics. For example, the word origins suggest it is appropriate for an alderman (or -woman) to talk about what happens on his or her *watch*.

The reader will find a section on swearing, not intended to encourage it, but simply to understand how one person's four-letter curse is another

Introduction

person's healthy, emotional outlet. *Bastard* and *bitch* were thought too shocking to put in the newspaper until recently. Not now. A few years ago a *Wizard of Id* comic-strip character called the king a *bugger*. No problem in the United States, but in Canada the word had to be changed to the less vulgar *beggar*. Today, even on radio and television, you'll hear words you didn't hear a decade ago. It's true that censorship is anathema — we recall the ludicrous depredations of the notorious Dr. Bowdler and his censorious daughter.

The escalation of foul language in Hollywood's films makes one wonder how they will make a dramatic, street-talk point in the future when we are no longer shocked by the expectoration of four-letter words. Just as special-effect chases, crashes, and explosions have replaced classic dramatic form (conflict, climax, denouement, and so on), gutter language is a no-brainer approach to writing what passes for dialogue. Check Shakespeare. What were his expletives? *Forsooth* and *zounds*! Is it just that we grew accustomed to them and now think them simply archaic and cute?

Spoonerisms (metatheses) and Oxford's remarkable Doctor Spooner get some attention in these pages, too, along with puns, limericks, and word puzzles.

FOREIGN WORDS

For some major languages, this guide offers tips on the pronunciation of consonants, vowels, and combinations. And it gives guidance on where the emphasis usually falls. Languages covered in some detail include Chinese, French, German, Italian, Portuguese, Russian, Swedish, and Spanish. Learn the rules and you will seldom be stumped by a new foreign word or name. (See Appendix B.)

- *Genoa* is said **JEN-o-ah**, not **jin-O-uh** (as heard on a Toronto TV newscast).
- *Toronto* is said **tuh-RAWN-toe**, not **TRAWNA**.
- *Bordelaise* is said **bor-d'LEZ**.

For some other major language groups, or countries such as Turkey, India, the islands of the Pacific, a few hints and tips are offered. Many foreign place names can be found in gazetteers or in the Geographical Section of the *Webster Collegiate Dictionary*. Many names and words are transliterated using the sound values of European languages such as English, French, Italian, Spanish, German, or Portuguese. In some cases the transliteration depends on which of the old imperial powers was once in authority. Even Chinese and Japanese names are spelled out in English phonetics.

WORDS, WORDS, WORDS

> *For words, like nature, half reveal,*
> *And half conceal the soul within....*
> — Lord Tennyson

An alphabetical list of commonly misused words attempts to help the reader avoid most embarrassing errors in everyday speech. It is a list to build on while one checks the dictionary regularly. It's a list to consult when in doubt about conflicting meanings of words such as *career* and *careen*, or *poutine* and *poteen*. It is a fun trivia list to check for usage questions like that of *bacterium* versus *bacteria*. And it's a list to explore for pronunciation of words like *access, flaccid,* and *succinct*.

Another list offers guidance on pronunciation of personal and geographical names. Yet another alphabetical list deals with some Latin, Greek, and other foreign terms and phrases. And there's a list of musical terms and names, too. Check for Purcell and Puccini. While these are helpful lists, it is not the intention of this book to be a comprehensive pronouncing dictionary. This volume is an aid to avoiding common traps of mispronunciation or misuse.

VIVA VOCE: VOICE AND PRESENTATION

A chapter on presentation deals with organization of material. It offers an armature on which to build content systematically. It discusses the "proem," the "Three Tell System," and the "Rule of Three" for telling humorous stories. It also touches on semantics, phrasing, breathing, and other presentation considerations. In addition, this section discusses the human voice and how to use it. It examines briefly the chore of recording narration. Some tongue twisters round out the chapter, inviting you to trip the light fantastic, linguistically speaking.

Included is a short chapter on broadcast journalism, offering some standard preparation and style tips. "Father Murphy's Ass" takes an irreverent look at how perspective and brevity can distort a headline; how literal fact can be twisted into bias. This chapter considers the need for an informed public and the role of the media in a democracy. Public attitudes are also considered, along with the issue of news as entertainment. In addition to the issue of the trivialization of news, the media section touches on editing and on the demand for brevity and drama in "sound bites." But broadcasting is a business with a prime interest in the profit line, so it comes as no surprise that compromises are made in business-news reporting and even in language use in order to please sponsors. This chapter also argues that public broadcasters have a special responsibility, not just to inform, but to demonstrate a love of good speech.

Introduction

Nyms, Phobes, and Philes

Is it a "phalanx of prostitutes" or "a pride of loins"?

Included is a section on *-nyms* of various kinds, such as antonyms, eponyms, homonyms, synonyms, and acronyms. This section also deals with *-phobes* and *-philes* (hates and loves). There are lists of prefixes and suffixes, useful in figuring out meanings or whether words are legitimate though unfamiliar. This chapter also tackles common singular-versus-plural difficulties and the amusing problem of collectives. When "ladies of the night" congregate, it isn't always in a seraglio or bordello[3].

Effective communication requires clarity. Distractions of accent, speech peculiarities, or any affectation get in the way. We hope to be immediately understood. But sometimes we are tempted to use words for show, to appear erudite. If we use a term incorrectly, however, we convince the listener of our ignorance. It's better to aim for simple, direct connection and understanding. To paraphrase Churchill, the old and simple words are best. The appropriate adages are "Less is more," and the KISS formula, "Keep It Simple, Stupid." *The Elements of Style* by Strunk and White makes the point effectively. It is as valuable a guide to clear writing as any text ever written, as valuable as any good dictionary.

Time changes all things, including spellings and pronunciations. One of the beauties of English is that it is flexible and adaptable. It welcomes new words. It accepts new meanings for old words. Popular usage imposes new ways of saying things. *Gay* once meant light-hearted, filled with fun. Its sexual-orientation meaning makes some of the song lyrics of just a few decades ago seem quite silly. And there are fads in words and usage. Jazz trumpet players once talked about their embouchures as their "chops." Now players of stringed instruments, too, and even dancers talk about their chops when they refer to their skills. The language is always in a state of flux. And not just English. *Flamenco* comes from an Andalusian word (meaning "Flemish") applied to the Jews returning from banishment in Flanders. They had fled there after the defeat of the Muslims in southern Spain, when the monarch imposed Catholicism on everyone. The term came to be applied to a lifestyle, to music, and to a freewheeling dance on the margins of respectability.

Standards

While language is always changing, there are norms. Without standards, English would not have become the lingua franca of our time. So, while we avoid rigidity, it helps if we acknowledge standards of educated usage which find common ground and preserve meaning. Carelessness can lead to misunderstanding and unintended humour:

You Can Say That Again!

ENRAGED COW INJURES FARMER WITH AXE

PLANE TOO CLOSE TO GROUND, CRASH PROBE INDICATES

STUDY FINDS SEX, PREGNANCY LINK

TWO SISTERS REUNITED AFTER 18 YEARS IN CHECKOUT LINE

COLD WAVE LINKED TO TEMPERATURES.

It is bothersome enough that the language is always changing and that, during change, meanings can be ambiguous. Naturally this hampers understanding. It is well worth the effort, therefore, to stick with the common, current, educated pronunciation and meaning.

Some argue that caring about correct pronunciation and use is elitist, even a form of snobbery. They argue that common, everyday speech is democratic, the language of "everyman." This is the argument of the careless populist versus the elitist, pedantic snob.

But people who care about communicating effectively and gracefully will defend the language against careless abuse. Anyone who mounts a podium has a duty to use the language with care. Theirs is a leadership role. Those in the media have a special responsibility. Too many broadcasters seem to feel they know it all without checking a dictionary or thesaurus. Or perhaps they really feel the popular speech of the street serves well enough. Each of us favours the pronunciation and speech habits we learned as we grew up. These habits were formed within a family culture, in our ethnic environment, and in the cultural stratum in which we moved. Our prejudice is that, if our habits aren't the universal standard, they are at least "normal" and anything else is "putting on airs."

One excuse the electronic media may have is that educators don't set a high-enough standard. Latin is no longer obligatory, not even one year of it, so the foundation is weaker. New styles of language are popularized in film, television comedy, and the advertising industry. So a special effort is required from teachers and from the media in order to maintain a standard of speech superior to that of the careless vernacular of the street.

It is fair to argue that English is malleable and that this is one of its great advantages. We might even accept the argument that the short form *Inc.*, once read as *incorporated*, is often pronounced "INK" these days. Perhaps the advertising writers and pop-speak advocates have won that one, just as *corp.* (said **KORP**) threatens to replace *corporation*. And add

30

Introduction

KO for *company* to the list. But *irregardless* is still wrong. It is not a word. *Regardless* will do. And *notorious* still has a negative connotation, as does *infamous,* in spite of common misuse. Neither word is simply a synonym for *famous* or *well-known.*

SOUNDS LIKE

A common error is to treat English as a phonetic language and to pronounce every syllable as valuable. So we hear *vegetable* said "VEJ-et-AB-ul" instead of "VEJ-ta-bul." Or *listener* is sometimes pronounced LIS-ten-ir instead of LIS-nir. Some people even introduce vowel sounds that don't exist, turning *athlete* into ATH-ul-eet or *jewelry* into JOO-el-ir-ee instead of JOOL-ree and saying FIL-um instead of FILM. The truth is, we're often correct when we drop syllables: *Wednesday* is said WENZ-day.

As to words and names from other languages, *Paris* is PAR-is and not puh-REE. The latter is clearly an affectation in English context. Sportscasters are fond of saying MO-ray-al kan-aj-YENZ, affecting a French pronunciation for the "Habs" but often mispronouncing the names of French Canadian players. In Canada, in English, *Trois-Rivières* is officially traw-riv-YAIR but *Montreal* is mun-tree-AWL and not mow-ray-AWL. *The Pas* in Manitoba is thuh PAW, *Sault Ste. Marie* is SOO sint mar-EE. And the main intersection in downtown Winnipeg is Portage (POR-tij) and Main. Canadian place names (as is true in the United States for names originally French or Spanish) present a problem. Some get full French value. Others have been anglicized to some degree.

They are many words of French origin in English and others little changed from their Latin origins. Most of them have been anglicized and can be considered English words. Returning to a French pronunciation for *valet* or *homage* or *sorbet* is just an affectation, but it has acquired some *cachet* (ka-SHAY). It is a matter of vogue. It is not incorrect for an English speaker to say VAL-et or SOR-bit in an English context. The motion picture industry in Hollywood likes to say o-MAWZH (*homage*). They seem to think it's sophisticated. The English word is said HAW-mij or AW-mij. In the same category is *penchant*. It is an English word in an English context and said PEN-ch'nt. It may not be wrong to say pawn-SHAWN, but it is putting on airs. The problem is, some words from French have been thoroughly and correctly anglicized while others are still said with an approximation of the French. We still pronounce *fait accompli* as "fet a-kawm-PLEE." For *noblesse oblige* we say "no-BLES o-BLEEZH." With the term for treason or taking liberties, *lèse majesté*, we even retain the grave accent on the *e* in the first word and the acute accent over the final *e* in most English renderings of the term pronounced "lez mazh-es-TAY." *Contretemps* is another instance of adoption of a foreign word with the original pronunciation retained.

We should stick with popular anglicized usage unless the word is commonly pronounced in the manner of indigenous usage as in *Worcester*, **WOO-stir**, or *Leicester*, said **LES-tir**. A street in downtown Toronto, *Breadalbane,* is often mispronounced **BRED-il-BANE**, when it should be **bruh-DAWL-bin**. *Balliol*, another Toronto street, is locally pronounced **buh-LOIL** and seldom **BAL-ee-ul** as at the college in England.

Some names have two correct pronunciations. In the United States, *Arkansas* is pronounced **AR-kin-SAW** when it's the state but **ar-KAN-zis** when it's the river. Back to Toronto, where the street is *Spadina*, said **spuh-DY-nah**, while the mansion near Casa Loma is called **spu-DEEN-uh**. *Dalhousie* University in Halifax is pronounced **dal-HOWZ-ee**. The port in Ontario near Niagara is pronounced **duh-LOOZ-ee**. For foreign names, check the index to determine the country and the language and then check Appendix B for phonetic guidance. Clearly, we shouldn't make snap assumptions based on the spelling. It pays to check. Not just names, but even English words we think we know.

Under the heading of troublesome English words, this guide takes sides on some issues but not on others. So the word *harass* is **HAR-us** and not **huh-RASS**. The jury is still out on that one, especially in the United States. And it is hard to tell which side is winning on the *kilometre* issue. **KIL-o-ME-tur** is clearly correct if you stick with the meaning: a thousand metres. There is no reason it should rhyme with *thermometer*, but **kil-AWM-i-tir** threatens to become common. *Often* is said **AWF-in**. *Expertise* is said **ex-pur-TEEZ**, not **ex-pur-TEES**. In Canada, *foyer* is pronounced **FOY-ay**.

With some words there is no tolerance for even popular mispronunciation. For instance, you "*plumb the depths of something.*" The word *plumb* means "the lead weight on the end of a line" (Fr. *plomb*). Samuel Clemens took his *nom de plume* (pen name) from the practice of *plumbing* the depths of the Mississippi to avoid running the paddlewheel boats aground. "Mark twain!" (two) was the shout to the captain to let him know how deep or shallow the river was. *Plummet,* on the other hand, means "to fall" — nothing to do with lead or plumb. *Succinct* is said **suk-SINKT** (not **sus-INK**). And, while "to err is human, to forgive divine," it is not said **AIR** but **IR**, to rhyme with *fur* or *sir*.

The goal is speech that doesn't draw attention to itself by either error or affectation. Clean out the common dross from everyday speech and sound as though you know what you are talking about.

Above all, remember that as Confucius put it, "the whole end of speech is to be understood."

Introduction

1. *Larynx* (important to voice production, see Presentation) is pronounced **LAR-inks**, not **LAR-niks**.

2. In English there is no formal *you* pronoun as there is in other European languages (*tu* and *vous* in French). English once had the singular form (*thou, thee,* and *thine*) and the plural (*ye* and *you*). During the Middle Ages, the forms were used like *tu* and *vous*. Gradually the polite plural, *you,* was more widely used and the distinction was devalued. *You* was used to address everyone, regardless of status and number. Soon *thou* was less common, surviving only in prayers.

3. *Seraglio* is derived partly from the Turkish *saray* (palace). *Sarayli* means "woman of the palace." The Latin *serrare* (to lock) also contributed, yielding *seraglio* (**sir-AL-yo**): "women's quarters." *Bordello* comes from Italian and, originally, from the Old French word *bordel* (small farm). *Harem* is from Arabic *haram* for "a prohibited place" or "sanctuary."

QUIZ 1
?

1) What does *fiera* mean in Spanish? _____

2) Mark the syllable which gets the heaviest emphasis in *decorative.*

3) Mark the syllable in *Genoa* that gets the heaviest accent _____

4) The word *flamenco* came to Spain from _____

5) Write the following phonetically: *schism, Paris, listener, err,* and *deter.*

For answers, see Appendix A.

CHAPTER ONE

Pronunciation

CHAPTER ONE

Pronunciation

Speech is civilization itself.
— Thomas Mann

One good reason for improving the way we speak is to communicate more effectively. Another is to make a good impression. Even if we use an informal, non-standard vernacular for everyday purposes, a better, "Sunday best" suit of clothes is helpful on special occasions. Some make the effort for career enhancement. Others simply want to set a good example for their children. We are fortunate if our parents speak well. And we're blessed if we have an influential teacher or two.

The spoken word is a valuable social tool. Its prehistoric invention required some agreement on the meanings of sounds or combinations of sounds. Our ancestors had to agree on how to say consistently a certain sound or set of sounds. Then, presumably, they agreed on how they would arbitrarily apply their invented words to particular things or events. We still make those tacit agreements. If we didn't, we wouldn't be able to communicate.

With writing we try to represent the sounds of words. But the evolution of writing and our ever-changing spoken language make it necessary to devise another system, one that will accurately represent the sounds we make when we speak. That sound system is phonetics. Syllable by syllable we break words into sound elements and represent them in order. *Phonetic* becomes **fo-NET-ik**. *Language* becomes **LANG-wij**. *Invention* becomes **in-VEN-tshun**. These examples use a simple form of phonetics. There are others capable of far greater accuracy and subtlety, but in these pages we work with common English sound values with the stressed syllable in upper case.

This chapter explores several systems used to represent the sounds of speech. Some attention is also given to copy preparation, syllabification, and accenting or emphasis. Phrasing and breathing are important too, because ideas are conveyed by combinations of words or sounds. Break a sentence in the wrong place and you change its meaning or even render it meaningless. We have to hear word groupings, phrases, and clauses in order to understand what is being said. We hear inflection variety as well. We hear ideas, pictures, and feelings.

So it matters a lot where you breathe. The song lyric "What is this thing called love?" shows how the same words mean very different things, depending on the rhythm, the inflection, the phrasing, and the emphasis. "What *is* this thing called, love?" "What is *this* thing called love?" "What is this *thing* called love?" "What is this thing *called*, love?" And, "What is this thing called *love*?"

FORMAL, INFORMAL

A cultivated speaker uses a different standard in a public speech than he employs in everyday conversation around the water cooler. In rapid and informal discussion the words *has*, *him*, and *his*, unless specially stressed, lose their *h*'s. The *t* disappears from combinations like *must go*, *sit down*, *next day*, and so on. They become phonetically *mus'go, siddown, nex'day*. Many words have two levels of pronunciation, stressed and unstressed. Stress can change a pronunciation or even influence the dropping of a sound. "Did you talk to him?" could be "Did you TALK to 'im?" And that's still acceptable speech. For another meaning, it could be "Did you talk to HIM?" In this case, the word *him* gets full value because we want to know if a particular person was consulted. These distinctions convey meaning. Elisions and contractions are okay. On the other hand, not so acceptable is the question "Dijatawktum?"

The appropriate degree of formality in speech varies from setting to setting, whether it be the public platform, popular broadcasting, the boardroom, a seminar, or a casual dinner. If we acknowledge that we make these distinctions all the time, perhaps we won't feel self-conscious when we choose to "speak *up*" when asked to make post-prandial remarks from the head table or make the team's presentation in the corporate boardroom. "Cultivated formal" is the speech standard used for special, formal occasions, a eulogy for instance. "Cultivated informal" is the speech we hear most of the time on radio and television — except, of course, in some sitcoms. To illustrate our willingness to alter our speech — including our grammar and even voice production — to suit the occasion, consider the politician who inserts a little of the vernacular, sometimes even mild expletives, in order to sound more down-to-earth and ingratiate himself with a particular segment of the electorate. Appropriateness is an important consideration. But there are risks in cutting your vocal cloth to suit the situation. The politician might be considered a phony if the performance is unconvincing. A white politician is a fool to try to speak Ebonic English.

And then there are dialects. A dialect is not just a provincial deviation, but a combination of characteristics peculiar to a place or social group. Each of us has a unique dialect reflecting influences that began when we were in the cradle.

Pronunciation

"Standard" and "non-standard" are terms used to describe speech considered "socially acceptable." "Standard" is usually applied to the speech of educated people in the community. In England the term "received pronunciation" is used rather than "standard." It is the speech heard in upper-crust London, and it has been encouraged in prestigious schools and universities. This is not to condone the lisp, the *w* for *r*, or the stuttering affectations of some Britons who wish to be mistaken for landed gentry. In North America there are local and regional variations and some of them are preferred. But no barrier to communication exists, except perhaps in the case of so-called Black English, which is understood only within its own narrow social confines. Perhaps it can be compared with the French *joual* in Quebec.[1]

Another way to make the speech distinction is to contrast "cultivated" with "folk" speech. Many regional differences are disappearing, as a kind of universal English takes over with the help of television and film.[2]

There is still a distinctly Canadian speech. There's no question, the British influence was pervasive for a long time. More recently Canadians have been greatly exposed to American speech and usage. The Americanization of Canadian speech is like a flood. But, while Canadian English may have a lot in common with American and British speech, there are still some distinctions we can make.

The similarities of American and Canadian English are not surprising because the British Isles are the common source. After the American Civil War, the influx of United Empire Loyalists into Canada maintained the similarities. Later, British and American immigration reinforced the habits of speech brought to Canada previously. And standards preserved in Ontario schools moved west when Ontarians headed to the Prairies and the West Coast.

Americans say they can tell a Canadian from an American by the pronunciation of *house* or *out and about*. What they hear is what's called "Canadian Raising," a term used to describe the non-lowering of some diphthongs usually lowered in other dialects. The tongue is raised higher for the diphthong in *knife* and *house* than in *knives* and *houses*. "Canadian Raising" is quite common in Montreal, Toronto, Ottawa, Vancouver, and Victoria. But the trend is away from raising toward more American values, so *cot* and *caught* often sound the same, as do *don* and *dawn, caller* and *collar*. We increasingly hear the same vowel sound in all of the words in these examples. That's the way Americans say these words, except in places near the Canadian border.

"T-flapping" and "T-deletion" are two tendencies common to many Canadians and Americans. A lot of Canadians say *t* as *d* between vowels and after *r*. That is, *waiting* and *wading* sound alike, as do *latter* and *ladder*, and *hearty* and *hardy*. The phrase "put the pedal to the metal" usually sounds more like "put the pedal to the **medal**." Ottawa is often said "Oddawa" (**AWD-i-waw**). Too often Toronto is said "Torrona" or "Trawna."

There are instances of distinctive Canadian word usage, such as the use of *tap* in some places rather than *faucet*. *Porch* and *verandah*, and *pail* versus *bucket* further illustrate these vocabulary distinctions. The variants aren't exclusively American or Canadian — some words are just more likely to be heard in Canada than in the States. Similarly, more Canadians are likely to say *lever, schedule, aunt, route, hostile, mobile*, and *missile* differently than most of their American cousins. Canadians say **LEE-ver** (lever). Canadians more often say **BEEN** rather than **BIN**, while *anti-*, *semi-*, and *multi-* rhyme with *me* in Canada, while *mobile* and *missile* rhyme with *Nile*, rather than the American *ill*.

Canadians also enjoy an indigenous vocabulary. From aboriginal roots come words like *toboggan, mukluk, mackinaw, anorak, parka, malamute*, and *husky*. From French come *mush* (*marcher*) and *toque* (**TOOK** or **TYOOK**). And, while most words of French origin have been anglicized over the centuries, Canadians unconsciously adopt French values in the pronunciation of many words. For instance, we say *garage* (**gar-AWZH**) differently from both Americans (**guh-RAJ**) and the British (**GAR-ij**). How long distinctively Canadian English will survive is anyone's guess. The tendency to Americanization is powerful.

PHONETICS

How do you say Groton? *For that matter, how do you say* Connecticut?

The city and state are pronounced **GRAW-tun, kuh-NET-i-KUT** (the first *c* in *Connecticut* is silent). As illustrated here, it is helpful, when dealing with unfamiliar words, to have a standard, convenient way to write the sounds. We need to know if an *a* is pronounced as in *hat* or as in *hate*. Is the symbol *e* pronounced as in *net*, or the letter *u* as in *nut* or as in *mute*? And, as with vowels, we need to know how the consonant sounds are indicated. Is a *c* said like *s* or like *k*?

To complicate matters, the sound values of some combinations of letters change. English is not consistent. Other languages have their own unique sounds for their alphabets. If French, Italian, Portuguese, and Spanish are phonetically consistent, English is not.[3]

Fortunately we have the International Phonetic Alphabet to help us record the sounds of the broad range of living languages and the variety of sometimes subtle differences not always immediately apparent to the unfocused ear. The phonetic system is a great aid for those who need to represent and reproduce vocal sounds with precision. But, for everyday use of non-linguists, we need a simpler system. Dictionaries such as the *Webster Collegiate* or the *Canadian Oxford* provide their own phonetic systems.

Pronunciation

Place names offer more examples of the value of phonetic guides:

- *Etobicoke,* the western suburb of Toronto, is pronounced **ih-TOE-bih-KO** (not **-KOKE**).
- *Lake Nipissing* is pronounced **NIH-pis-ing,** not **ni-PISS-ing**
- *Pictou County* in Nova Scotia is said **PIK-toe** (not **-too**).
- *Newfoundland* is pronounced **nyoo-f'nd-LAND.**
- *Brisbane,* Australia, is said **BRIZ-bin.**
- In Indiana, reflecting the influence of Canadian voyageurs from the St. Lawrence River valley, it's *Terre Haute* — **tair-ah HOTE.**

To avoid pronunciation errors we can make a habit of using the dictionary. We can learn the rules of our language and hope they will keep us on the rails, knowing all along that in English there are lots of exceptions. With place names, correct pronunciation is even more difficult than with other vocabulary. Move to a new part of the country or elsewhere in the world and there's a new list of place names to learn. Locals always enjoy teaching newcomers how to say local place names. In North America there are lots of place names not said as they are spelled.

LOOKS LIKE, SOUNDS LIKE

Fortunately there are guides simpler than the International Phonetic Alphabet. They work with a more limited range of sounds. The systems devised by the broadcast news wire services explain pronunciation by comparison with common English words and sounds. So we are told, for instance, that the French word *fait* (from the verb *faire,* "to make") rhymes with the English word *met* when followed by a word starting with a vowel. Thus we get the phonetic guide: *fait accompli* — **FET uh-kawm-PLEE.** (The *t* in *fait* is sounded because of the liaison with the word *accompli.*) Here, the emphasis or accented syllable is in upper case.[4]

The finely tuned dictionary phonetic systems use a (') symbol to show which syllable gets the emphasis and they often show both primary and secondary accent. In this book the syllable that gets the strongest emphasis is in **BOLD UPPER CASE.**

PHONEMES AND MORPHEMES

Aristotle was wrong to say the word is the smallest meaningful unit of speech, just as the atom was thought to be the smallest particle of matter. The "phoneme" is the smallest, sometimes meaningful, unit of speech. The *p* of *pat* is a phoneme. It is a sound but not necessarily a syllable. The minimal parts which convey meaning are "morphemes," like *map* or *mat*, linguistic units which contain no smaller meaningful components.

SOUNDS SIGNIFYING SOMETHING

The range of sounds in use varies from language to language. English has forty-five phoneme elements, including twenty-one consonants, nine vowels, three semi-vowels (*y, w, r*), four stresses, four pitches, one juncture (pause between words) and three terminal contours (inflections with which we end sentences). We are all familiar with the interrogatory upward inflection which enables us to turn a statement into a question. We also hear this inflection when the speaker appears to be asking for the listener's permission or agreement; it is not a very authoritative approach when it becomes a speech pattern — it undermines the speaker's credibility.

Languages include consonant sounds called "fricatives," "labials," "plosives" and so on. Some dialects of Arabic have twenty-eight consonants but only six vowels. Most African languages are like Mandarin and Burmese (Myanmar), using pitch and stress variation more than English does.

A "labial" is a sound made with the lips, like *f* or *p*. A "fricative" is a consonant made by the passage of air through a narrow aperture. Examples are *s, z, ah, zh, h, v, f, th*. "Plosive" sounds are characterized by the sudden forceful but brief passage of air. "Put the pen on the table, Tom," is an example of a plosive-laden sentence, likely to cause some "popping" on a microphone. The tongue twister "Peter Piper picked a peck of pickled peppers" is another case of *p*-popping plosives.

As young children discover, the loss of a front tooth can suddenly create a whistle or a lisp. A "sibilant" sound, except for the limited version necessary for saying *s* or *sh*, is to be avoided. It can be a problem for microphones and can annoy the listener. If nothing else, it's a distraction. Sometimes a hiss or a whistle is just a matter of carelessness or a bad habit. It can also be caused by the conformation of the teeth or even ill-fitting dentures. Or it may be an affectation, just as some people affect a *w*-sound for an *r*.

SCHWA

One problem occurring in pronunciation, and in representing spoken sounds with phonetic symbols, is the weak or obscured vowel as in the first syllable of the word *above* (**uh-BUV**). Sometimes the diminished vowel is situated at the end of a word; sometimes in the middle. In phonetics the *a* in *above* and the *e* in *often* are represented by the inverted *e* symbol called "schwa" which is found in dictionaries and in the

International Phonetic Alphabet. It is not used in this guide. Instead, the sound of the *a* in *about* is shown as **uh** (**uh-BOWT**). There are many instances of such indeterminate vowel sounds in our speech. Sometimes the appropriate representation changes, using other vowels with *h* to approximate the sound. In other cases you may find a vowel so diminished it is represented by an apostrophe to show there is something there but nothing that deserves much emphasis. *Vegetable* might be shown as **VEJ-tuh-b'l**. The point is that the vowel doesn't get full vocal value. It is almost lost and unheard, not critical to understanding. Whole syllables may disappear in correct speech, as in the name *Worcester* pronounced **WOO-stir**. If a vowel occurs in an unstressed syllable, it is pronounced as an obscure vowel, like *a* in *above*, the *o* in *consent*, or the *e* in *silent*. Keep in mind that it is not good speech to articulate and give full voice to every letter. It is good speech in many instances to lose some letters and occasionally whole syllables. The same is true for sentences said aloud rather than read. Whole words get little voice with emphasis being focused on the important ideas.

The International Phonetic Alphabet

This guide sets out to make it easier to come close to the sound values in a word or name. It isn't necessary to fine-tune the study to the point of using all the sounds represented by the symbols of the International Phonetic Alphabet. The simpler system, already in common use in media newsrooms, enables anchors to sound as though they know what they are talking about when dealing with foreign leaders and geography. When the simpler phonetics are in the script or on the teleprompter, the correct pronunciation is automatic with no interruption of flow, no embarrassing hesitation, nothing distracting the listener from the sense of the message. We will deal with that phonetic system — the one used in this book — after a closer look at the valuable International Phonetic Alphabet. For anyone serious about the nuances of accurate pronunciation, it is worth some study.

Symbols, Names, and Sounds

- (a)   front *a*, like English *a* in *man, can*.
- (ɑ)   back *a*, as in *father* or in the French *pâte*. This is the *a* usually heard in German, Italian, and Spanish.
- (ã)   nasal *a*, heard only in French: *en, genre*.
- (ʌ)   middle *a*, as in *funny*, or the *o* in *money*.
- (e)   closed *e*, like the *e* with acute accent in French.

(ɛ)   open *e* as in English *met*.

(ẽ)   nasal *e*, as in French *in*, *im*, or *en* after *i*.

(ǝ)   neutral *e* as in French *le*, *se*.

(i)   long *i* as in English *ski* or French *Mimi*.

(ɪ)   short *i* as in English *hit* or *bit*.

(j)   "yod," semi-consonant, like the *i* before *o* in *million*.

(o)   closed *o* as in English *rope* or French *au*, *eau*.

(O)   open *o* as in *port*, *sort*, *snort*.

(õ)   nasal *o* as in French *on*, *om*.

(u)   long *u* as in *food* or French *ou*, German *u* or *uh*.

(U)   short *u* as in *foot*.

(w)   semi-consonant of *u*, as in the French *oui*.

(y)   French or umlaut *u* for the vowel *u* in the French *tu*.

(ɤ)   semi-consonant of French *u* as before the vowel in *puis*.

(ø)   closed *eu* as in French final sound (-*euse* ending).

(œ)   open *eu* as in French *eu* when followed by a consonant (*pneu noir*, *pleut plus*).

(aj)   a yod diphthong[5] like *y* in *sky*.

(aw)   like *ow* in English *meow*, French diphthong *aou* as in *caoutchouc*.

(ʌw)   diphthong of middle *a* and of *u* as in English *ouch*.

(ɑw)   diphthong of back *a* and of *u* like *ow* as in *plow*.

(Oj)   diphthong of *O* and yod like English *oy* as in *boy*.

(ij)   diphthong of long *i* and yod as in French *ille*.

(_j)   diphthong of open *eu* and yod, French: *eu* + *il*, *ille*.

(b)   English *b* in *bee*.

(d)   French *d* as in *dent*, Italian *Dante*.

(dz)   English j as in *budget*, Italian *gioconda* (**jo-KON-da**).

(f)   f ("eff") as in French *fier* or *photo* or German *Vater*.

(g)   hard *g* as in French *gu* (*g* + *a*, *o*, *u*).

(h)   h ("aitch").

(z)   French *j* as in English *leisure* or French *joli*.

(k)   "kay," French *c*, *k*, *cc*, *ch*, *qu* or German *k*, *ch*, *ck*, final *g*, Italian and Spanish *c* + *a*, *o*, *u*.

(x)   "khy," *ch* in Scottish *loch*.

(ç)   German *ch* with *e*, *i*, *ei*, *l*, *r*.

(ñ)   "nyay," *ny* in *canyon*, French *mignon*, Italian *Mascagni*.

(ŋ)   "ing," *ng* as in *sing*.

(p)   "pea," *p*, *pp*, *ph* and a final *b* in German.

(r)   "arr" for the single **r**, however it is spelled.

(s)   "ess" like *s* in English *astronomer*.

(ʃ)   "shay" like the *sh* in the English word *shave*.

(t)   "tee" for French or German *t*, *tt*, *th*.

(c)   alternate symbol for "chay."

(tʃ)   "chay," like *ch* in *church*.

44

(ð)   voiced *th* as in English *them*. Note that this differs from *th* in *thin*.

(θ)   unvoiced *th* or "theta" as in Castilian[6] *c* + *e* or *i*.

(v)   "vee."

(z)   "zed" as French *z*, intervocalic *s*; German initial and medial *s*; Italian intervocalic *s*.

A SIMPLE GUIDE TO PRONUNCIATION (pruh-NUN-see-AY-shun)

Broadcast-newsroom phonetic systems developed over time and work as instant guides to the pronunciation of difficult words and names. The trouble is, no two newsroom systems are alike. An anchor may not be able to understand another writer's symbols. An editor's attempt to help an anchor or reporter could lead to misunderstanding and a fumble on the air. And mispronunciation sticks out like the proverbial sore thumb. It distracts. Worse, it undermines understanding and credibility. That's why Broadcast News (CP) has developed a consistent system.

The broadcaster is concerned with sounds. Who cares if there's a spelling error as long as the intended word is heard? It's more important that the listener or viewer knows by sound what was said. Can the reader break up the word into syllables and give each one its due? Can the aid be written in above the line or in parenthesis and upper case after the troublesome name? If the letters come from a language other than our own, can we approximate the sounds they convey? Are there any rules to help us come close to a correct accent and sound?

In most cases it is wise to check a dictionary or some other authority. The phonetic guidance system used is a matter of personal preference. Use the International Phonetic Alphabet if you wish to reproduce the full range of subtle sound differences in a number of tongues. Or, if you prefer, use the system in your dictionary or one you devise for yourself. If you want to come close but aren't concerned with the nuances, you can use this guide:

Vowels:

a	*a* as in *hat, marry*.
ay	*a* as in *late, plate*.
ah	*a* as in *father*.
aw	*a* as in *law*.
e	*e* as in *ebb, set, merry, next*.
ee	*e* as in *feet, feat*.
i	*i* as in *hit, big*.
y	*i* as in *wine*.
	y as in *by*.

o	*o* as in *oats*.
oo	*o* as in *poor*.
aw	*o* as in *not, ox*.
ow	*o* as in *loud*.
u	*u* as in *up*.
yu, yoo	*u* as in *news, beauty*.

Consonants:

b	*b* as in *bat*.
c	*c* as in *bacillus*.
ch	*ch* as in *church, cha-cha*.
d	*d* as in *do, rudder*.
f	*f* as in *fit, differ*.
g	*g* as in *get, beg, trigger, give*.
h	*h* as in *hit, hear, behave*.
j	*g* or *j* as in *just* or *fudge, gesture*.
k	*k* or *c* as in *kiss, Quebec, cocoon*.
l	*l* as in *low, all*.
m	*m* as in *my, him*.
n	*n* as in *now*.
p	*p* as in *pot*.
r	*r* as in *read*.
s	*s* as in *see*.
sh	*s* as in *shoe*.
t	*t* as in *ten*.
th	*th* as in *thin*.
v	*v* as in *vice*.
w	*w* as in *west*.
y	*y* as in *yes, lawyer*.
	N.B.: **y** may also represent the long *i* as in *by, wine* (see **vowels** above).
z	*z* as in *zeal* or *zenith*, or *those*.
zh	*s* as in *vision, derision*.

As mentioned, good speech sounds natural and unaffected. Some letters aren't even sounded. Sometimes whole syllables go missing when a word is said aloud. And elisions which run the end of one word into the start of another are natural and acceptable.

And, while we're at it, contractions are encouraged. *Cannot* should be *can't*. *Will not* is preferably *won't*. On the other hand, we should pronounce *-ing* endings and not permit sloppiness to creep into our speech. But we should recognize that it's natural to make some compromises when we translate from writing to speech.

Pronunciation

Emphasis is also part of what we hear. *Where* the stress falls in a word helps us recognize and understand. So, when we are writing a phonetic aid for ourselves, we need to come close to the appropriate emphasis, especially when pronouncing a foreign name or word. First we break the word into syllables or parts that sound like syllables to us.

Some languages usually put the accent on the final syllable. This is the case in French. The verb *revenir* is said "**ruh-v'-NEER**."

In other languages — like Japanese — the syllables seem to the Western ear to have almost equal emphasis, and intonation is used to vary meaning of similar sounds and sound combinations. Of course, with Japanese, we have used English sound values for the transliteration. Our attempts to represent Japanese values phonetically are crude approximations, as in *sukiyaki* — **soo-kee-YA-kee**, or *Nagano* — **NAG-an-o**. Sometimes the Western ear hears an accented syllable where there is none.

Once a word is divided into parts, the next move is to find out what sound is indicated by each letter or combination of letters. For instance:

Gianni Schicchi	gi/ann/i schi/cchi	**JAWN-ee SKEE-kee**
succinct	suc/cinct	**suk-SINKT**
fromage	fro/mage	**fro-MAWZH**
wunderbar	wun/der/bar	**VOON-der-bar**

In French and other Romance languages, once you know the value of individual letters, you can put vowels together to come up with sounds which may be difficult at first for those whose mother tongue is English. Unlike English, *la belle langue* is actually phonetic. For instance, the usually mispronounced name of the great NHL star Mario Lemieux is not **le-MYOO** as most commentators have said it. The last syllable is a combination of *i* (**ih**), *e* (**eh**), *u* (**oo**) (a three-vowel diphthong, if that weren't a contradiction in terms) run together to give us **-MYUH**. This is a crucial demonstration. Once you know the sound values, whatever the language, you can figure out how to say the word.

Sport stars accept popular mispronunciations of their names. The Russians, Swedes, Czechs, Italians, and French Canadians playing in the National Hockey League accept the often clumsy, sometimes cavalier, treatment of their names. Some sportscasters pride themselves on getting the pronunciation right. Others seem to take a perverse (if not xenophobic) pride in mangling names. Until sometime in 1998 Don Cherry was unable to manage goalie Patrick Roy's name on "Hockey Night In Canada," and usually said it to rhyme with *boy*.[7]

This isn't good enough in most situations. For the majority of us, our name is an important part of who we are. When it is mispronounced, we are offended. When listeners hear a speaker mispronounce a name, they lose confidence in the source. And they are distracted. When broadcasters — especially news anchors — get names wrong they lose credibility. For some that's not important. Many commentators get paid by the rant, not for being correct. (Some get paid for rant *and* for being *right*, but that's an ideological arrangement.)

PREPARATION

As the smooth old pros know, it pays to read copy in advance. This isn't always possible, so some politicians, after-dinner speakers, and broadcasters pride themselves on their ability to "lift it off the paper" when reading it "cold."

Some business executives do themselves a disservice and inflict pain on their staff by regularly presenting unfamiliar material at meetings. Even the most skilled readers are wise to do themselves and their audience the favour of quietly and privately reading the copy aloud before a presentation.

A lot of politicians consider themselves orators when they are not. Politicians often depart from scripts prepared for them and wander into culs-de-sac of their own creation. A malapropism or mispronunciation here and there is of little consequence — they think. But voters may turf the rascals out eventually, just because they find them embarrassing.

The "rip and read" school of broadcasting is risky — mistakes are inevitable. Typographical errors are common and they can lead a reader out onto a meaningless limb where recovery is almost impossible. There is enough "seat of the pants" flying in broadcast news without adding to its unpredictability. Even with one's own copy it is wise to prepare. Now that many broadcast teams no longer prepare complete hard copy for readers but depend on computerized prompters on air, it is especially wise to read everything over in advance. And, when a politician, company spokesperson, or after-dinner speaker is going to be reading someone else's copy, it's doubly important that the speech is read over in advance and aloud — into a tape recorder if possible.

Attention to copy preparation soon becomes a habit and the pronunciation rules for major languages quickly become second nature.

Examine the copy for thoughts, the phrasing, and the words. Read the material aloud. Print the phonetics above the line if possible. Do it syllable by syllable so there will be no dread, no surprise, no doubt, and no interruption of the flow when the text is read aloud.

Pronunciation

(zyoo-GAN-awv)
The <u>arrival</u> of <u>Syuganov</u>, / the <u>Communist candidate</u>
for the <u>Russian</u> <u>Presidency</u> / attracted a <u>large crowd,</u>/
<u>shouted down </u>by....

Not only is the proper name phonetically indicated, but the key thoughts are underlined. The articles, conjunctions, and prepositions are little more than spacers in oral/aural communications. There is a difference between the grammar of print and the grammar of vocal presentation. Grammar and punctuation can be pedantic in speech. As a rule, neglect articles, conjunctions, and prepositions. Sometimes even a verb is little more than a link between ideas as is the case of the first two uses of *is* in this sentence. Don't emphasize such a verb. Give it little voice.

Some broadcasters say *the* to sound like **thee** when it is unnecessary. *The* is said **thuh** (schwa) in most contexts unless the following noun begins with a vowel or when the article requires special emphasis to make a distinction.

The same goes for *and* as well as other conjunctions and prepositions, unless special emphasis is needed. For instance, you may need to distinguish *to* versus *from,* or *in* from *out.* But normally they get only secondary or tertiary emphasis.

In vocal presentation many words fall through the cracks — and so they should. It is not good speech to pronounce every syllable or give them equal weight. It is not good speech to give words equal voicing. The placement of emphasis is essential to the understanding of a text. Inappropriate emphasis is a common sin among poorly trained broadcasters today. They may argue that this is their style, but they are simply misguided. Read the following sentence aloud, giving heavier emphasis to the **bolded** words:

> **If** you can, take a ride **on** the train **and** drink in **the**
> inspiring beauty **of** the Rocky **Moun**tains.

This is an example of inappropriate emphasis on words which convey little meaning. It is an unnatural way to read the sentence. The following emphasizes the words that are essential to meaning:

> If you can, / **take** a **ride** on the **train** / and **drink** in the
> **inspiring beauty** / of the **Rocky Mountains.**

If you were to read only the bolded words to a listener, the meaning would be clear. Of course, inflection distinctions help too. Unfortunately too many broadcasters develop a speech pattern. It may become their signature sound. But it has the effect of undermining the sense of what they are reading. A singsong delivery — whether rhythm, or phrasing, or repeated inflection — can subvert the message. Inappropriate emphasis distorts. It can make it difficult for listeners to parse a sentence and extract the meaning as they listen. Remember, the spoken word is instant and ephemeral. Unlike the printed word, there is no second look.

PHRASING — MARKING COPY

Phrasing is the practice of grouping words together according to thought, fact, or idea. In the logic of oral presentation, articles and conjunctions have less importance. It is helpful to mark phrase groupings as we have done above. Natural breath control helps. And we mark for emphasis, too. This is the grammar of the way we speak.

Develop a marking scheme that works for you. It isn't necessary to adopt some arbitrary universal scheme. There really isn't one, except for the one used in music.

First and secondary emphasis can be distinguished by single and double underlining. Phrasing breaks can be marked with diagonals (/) as in the Syuganov example above. And sense groupings can be shown with curved musical-phrase brackets above the line of type. Some readers, narrators, actors, and commercial announcers use symbols for breath stops or pauses, differing according to the duration of the pause: /, //, ///, or / — /. Use ellipses (...) freely.

Volume can be marked as in music with *f, ff, fff* or *p, pp, ppp* for forte, fortissimo, or piano or pianissimo. Sometimes a **bold underline** will do.

And a line above the copy can show gradually increasing or decreasing volume. Or it might be used to indicate more or less voice (projection and resonance).

Symbols can be used to show a change of pace, acceleration, deceleration or even to remind the reader of a diminution in projection all the way down to a whisper. Some readers and news anchors use the brackets and other symbols from the standard keyboard as cues. Coloured highlighters can also be used. And font variation can be helpful too, especially to distinguish silent instructions from copy that is to be read aloud:

NEW LEAD — BRIGHTENER
A funny thing happened on the way to City Hall today where the mayor was to...

If you prepare copy with all the possible symbols mentioned here you probably won't be able to read it. The copy will be buried in an overburden of written-in cues. So be judicious. But, because of the time taken and the purposeful focus on the sense of the piece, you will have analyzed and parsed it enough to have almost memorized it. You will certainly understand it. And chances are your audience will understand it as you deliver your message.

The late John Drainie, one of Canada's greatest actors, always used his symbol system. Drainie was admired especially for the CBC Radio "Stage" series and for "The Investigator," in which he impersonated U.S. Senator Joseph McCarthy of anti-Communist, witch-hunt infamy. In early rehearsals and read-throughs Drainie's performance was wooden. Even in woodshed and dress rehearsal Drainie worked on his analysis. By air time his script was covered with what looked like fly specks. They were markings others couldn't read. But they made it possible for him to bring the script and character to life. When the red ON AIR light went on, Drainie was ready, in character, intense and convincing. He hardly needed the script for reference.[8]

BREATHING

There are two considerations in phrasing. The first is our need to breathe. The other is the importance of grouping words and sounds to convey units of sense. Marking those stops in advance helps us to read ahead.

"I sometimes think/ that/ never blows/ so red,
The rose/ as where/ some buried Caesar/ bled."

We automatically adjust our breathing and phrasing for sense. We should try to read about a line ahead of what we are saying. Whatever we do in preparation, however, should be done only to help us read naturally. We want what we read to sound like conversation.

Good speech, as we have already established, is not just a matter of giving precise vocal value to every letter in every syllable of every word. Elocution teachers once worked so passionately to correct sloppy speech that many people, including a lot of English teachers, concluded that the goal was to sound each syllable precisely. But what we really want in good speech is a natural combination of projection, appropriate inflection, resonance, intelligent phrasing, and correct but non-pedantic pronunciation. More about this in Chapter 9 on presentation.

The "elocutionists" weren't the only ones to take a puritanical and obsessively phonetic approach to speech. Early broadcasters wanted to set a standard. And they had to contend with the inadequacies of early transmission and receiving technology. Reception was often poor. The radios produced a poor approximation of the qualities of the human voice. And early microphones were, to put it charitably, primitive. So early broadcasters enunciated clearly. They spoke precisely and loudly. Early broadcast technology would not forgive sloppiness.

Broadcasters were careful to help the listener with very deliberate phrasing and correct pronunciation. And they projected, using their own, built-in amplification system to the fullest. That, and the staccato influence of the telegraph, gave early newscasters a punchy delivery. Among them was H. V. Kaltenborn, hammering out the news in New York in the early days of radio, converting the conventions of the newspaper of the day to a vocal equivalent. The newscasters barked out the news: "Good evening, ladies and gentlemen, and all the ships at sea...."

In London, the BBC set high standards right from the start but their care for the language and correct pronunciation did not mean an overly formal approach. And at the CBC, Canadian guardians of the language (like W. H. "Steve" Brodie) adopted the BBC approach — a not too formal one. They tried to keep their delivery conversational and natural, even on formal occasions like the broadcast description of a royal visit. All of this took place in an era before frequency modulation (FM), or digital, and much higher fidelity. Amplitude modulation, with extremely powerful transmitters like that of KDKA in Pittsburg, might produce sounds on farm fences but didn't promise a widespread, high-quality signal for the listener trying to pick it up with a cat's whisker crystal set.

As we have noted, English spelling is chaotic and unreliable. In French, some sounds can be represented by half a dozen spellings. Spanish is much more phonetically reliable. Italian is orthographically best, but the alphabet is inadequate for the full range of sounds. All these languages use an alphabet created by the Phoenicians and altered a bit by the Greeks. The Greeks learned to write sometime between 1000 and 700 B.C.[9] They converted a few superfluous signs for peculiarly Semitic consonants and invented others to express the vowel sounds which the Semites had ignored in their system. These vowel symbols are indispensable for the unambiguous expression of Indo-European language. It was apparently from Greek colonists in Italy that the Etruscans and Romans learned to read and write, but the Romans neglected to enhance the system enough to accommodate their own limited range of sounds. For western Europe, the Roman alphabet would have to do, even though it was to prove inadequate for the chore at hand.

The International Phonetic Alphabet, created by British phonetician Henry Sweet (1845—1912), may be the best. Anyone who is really serious about the study of pronunciation may want to learn it. Wire service transcriptions are much less reliable, but for practical purposes a similar, simple system is used in this book.

Another phonetic system is worth mentioning in passing. It's the one used by pilots and others communicating by radio in conditions where it is crucial that they be understood when interference or different languages might create doubt. People play fast and loose when spelling words over the phone, using any word that comes to mind. But there is a standard international system:

> Alpha, Bravo, Charley, Delta, Echo, Foxtrot, Golf, Hotel, India, Juliette, Kilo, Lima, Mike, November, Oscar, Papa, Quebec, Romeo, Sierra, Tango, Uniform, Victor, Whiskey, X-ray, Yankee, Zulu (sometimes Zebra).

A Canadian aircraft might identify itself as "Charley Hotel Oscar Quebec" (C–H–O–Q). Toronto International Airport is "Yankee Yankee Zulu" (Y–Y–Z).

To sum up to this point, we can say that after we've given full attention to the appropriate sounds for the language from which any given word is derived, after we've determined where the accent should fall, and after we've decided how to write the words phonetically, our goal is to sound natural. We want to be correct but we don't want to sound formal or contrived. Easy conversation is the sound we want.

The stentorian and ominous delivery of the narrators of *Movietone News*, the "voices of doom," prompts a giggle today. The best reader is the one who is almost invisible. Even among narrators and news anchors the goal is natural authority and credibility. The listener should not be conscious of style or method. The listener should simply be informed.

With that as our objective, it helps us to know our language origins and history. Knowledge of roots helps us use words correctly. It helps to know where we've come from linguistically.

SOME IMPORTANT TERMS AND SYMBOLS

Among the symbols that help us with pronunciation are those familiar from French: the **acute** accent (´), the **grave** accent (`), and the **circumflex** accent (^). Then there's the **cedilla** (ç) which turns a c from a k- into an s-sound. The **dieresis** or **umlaut** is found over the second of two vowels to indicate that the marked vowel gets separate pronunciation, as in *Noël* or *Citroën*. There's the ~ which we find over the first *n* in the Spanish word *mañana*. It tells us that the letter is pronounced like the *ny* combination in *canyon*.

Sometimes the word **nasal** is used to convey a sound value and not just as a derogatory comment on voice production. The nasal sound is heard in the French *maman*.

A **diphthong** is two vowels together in one syllable for a continuous sound as in *boy* or *sail*.

The **unvoiced consonants** are *c, f, h, k, p, s, sh, and t.* The **voiced consonants** are those to which we give sound from the throat (resonance): *b, d, g, j, l, m, n, r ,v, w, y, z.*

Elision (pronounced **el-IZH-un**) is the dropping of a vowel to aid the flow of speech as in *I'm* or *j'ai* (**ZHAY**).

Liaison is the joining of a normally silent final consonant to a word starting with a vowel, as in the French *mes amis* (**mayz-a-MEE**).

Stress is not just the nervousness experienced by the after-dinner speaker. It is also used to distinguish the relative force given to syllables in a word or phrase. The placement of the emphasis can determine the meaning of a sentence. Change the emphasis and you have changed the meaning, as we saw earlier with the song title "What is this thing called love?" The love song can become a joke through misplaced emphasis or stress. In a multisyllabic word the stressed sound is the one given the greatest emphasis (**EM-fas-is**). In many dictionaries the syllable getting the heaviest stress is preceded by '. A hyphen is generally used to separate syllables (syll-ab-if-ic-a-tion).

We also deal with **breath groups,** words grouped to make sense. Because they are linked on a single breath, they convey meaning, or concept, or relationship.

NOTES

1. **zhoo-AWL**, a dialectal way of saying *cheval* (horse). *Joual* borrows heavily from English; it has been somewhat legitimized by playwright Michel Tremblay and other Quebec writers.

2. McLuhan's "global village"?

3. Even the important "*e* before *i*" (and "*i* before *e*") rule is not invariably dependable, especially not in proper names. That is, *-ein* might be pronounced -EEN. Consider conductor Leonard Bernstein.

4. Do not confuse *fait* with *fête*. They may sound the same, but one means a "party" while the other is derived from the verb *to make*.

5. A diphthong is a speech sound in one syllable in which the sound starts as one vowel and changes to another (say *loud*). In phonetics the combined sequence of sounds is usually expressed with two or more symbols.

6. Castile: a region of central Spain, the source of standard and literary Spanish.

7. More on sports in the word list in Chapter 5.

8. For a page from a Drainie script for a *Jake and The Kid* performance see Bronwyn Drainie, *Living the Part* (1988).

Pronunciation

9. Before 300 B.C. an alphabet was expressing the sounds of the Aryan languages of India.

QUIZ 2
?

Indicate phonetically the pronunciation of:

1) *Groton, Connecticut* _____

2) *Pictou, Nova Scotia* _____

3) *St. John's, Newfoundland* _____

4) *Terre Haute, Indiana* _____

5) *Nipissing, Ontario* _____

6) Write phonetically the name of the International Phonetic Alphabet symbol for an obscured, or indistinct unstressed, vowel. _____
    What is it called? _____

7) Write phonetically the word *succinct.* _____

For answers, see Appendix A.

Chapter Two

In the Beginning Was ...

CHAPTER TWO

In the Beginning Was...

La, La, Poo, Poo

Language is the archives of history.
— Emerson

Caxton, the first English printer, wrote:

> And certaynly our language now used varyeth ferre from that which was used and spoken when I was borne. For we englysshe men ben borne under the domynacyon of the mone, which is never stedfaste, but ever waverynge, wexynge one season, and waneth and decreaseth another season.

Language does not stand still. Sleep for a few years like Rip Van Winkle and you might have trouble understanding people when you awake. Language is changing all around us all the time. We are seldom aware of how we alter our speech, adapting to fads and to changes in meaning and pronunciation.

World War II introduced as many as thirty thousand words into the highly defended French language. Some of those words have since been condemned, even driven out. Others, like *les blugines*, have survived, along with *le weekend* and *le snaquebarre*.[1] Wars cause language change. Short forms like *snafu* and *GI* and *WAVE* were born during wartime.[2] Technology makes a major contribution. *Boot* acquired another meaning with the computer. Cross-cultural influences are obviously another source of language change or enrichment.

Pronunciations change too. In Chaucer's time *house* and *bite* or *bight* would have rhymed with *goose* and *meet*. So, as Robert MacNeil, former anchor of the "MacNeil-Lehrer Report" on PBS, insisted in his *The Story Of English*, "Change is legitimate and inevitable, for our language is a mighty river, picking up silt and flotsam here and discarding there, but growing ever wider and richer."

In the present chapter we start where it all began, at least for major European languages and a few others. We listen briefly to the first intelligent sounds that evolved into useful symbols, sound symbols enabling us to say things to one another instead of just grunting, making a few signs and grimaces, and waving our arms in a frustrated semaphore. After reviewing the "la, la, poo, poo" theory, we consider Grimm's Law, which provides a model for vocal evolution. It is possible to trace words back through time and through a multitude of tongues.

Then we discover there is something fishy about the theory of Indo-European language origins. We take a look at the language family tree. Along the way it occurs to us there might be a way to come up with a universal spelling. That leads to the Esperanto solution. The proponents of a fundamentalist approach hope we will improve our speech with standard phonetic spelling.

Emerson said, "We are symbols and inhabit symbols." And perhaps Emerson was right. In any case, this chapter offers a fleeting look at semantics, another way to think about symbols, another reason to try to establish some sort of universal agreement that " a chair is a chair" even when the concept isn't broad enough to deal with all the different types of chairs. We recognize that the concept of snow is not specific enough to deal with all the different forms of snow experienced by the Inuit hunter in the Arctic.

Finally we'll revisit ancient Babylon and a towering ziggurat. As it is written in Genesis, *The whole earth was of one language and of one speech.* We will be in Babylon, the world's largest city, at the time the Persians were at its gates and when the prophet Daniel saw events as divine vengeance: *The Lord did there confound the language of all the earth...."*

"La la," "Poo poo," "Yo-he-ho," "Bow wow," and "Ma ma"

Herodotus wrote that the king of Egypt, Psamtik I, decided in 7 B.C. to find out what language children would speak if they had no one to teach them and when no language was spoken within their hearing.

Herodotus relates that Psamtik took two newborns and gave them to a shepherd to rear in complete isolation. After two years, the shepherd heard the children say "becos" repeatedly. It sounded like the word for bread in the language of the Phrygians. Psamtik assumed that was the first language ever spoken. It is likely the children were imitating sounds made by the shepherd's sheep.

Theories and guesses about the origins of speech include the "Bow wow" theory which proposes that the first language consisted of imitations of animal sounds. The "Yo-he-ho" theory argues that language derives from rhythmic chanting of people working together. The "La la" theory argues for music and song, especially associated with romance. Then there is the "Poo poo" theory, suggesting that the first words were instinctive sounds prompted by strong emotions like fear, anger, and pain. But nobody *knows* the origin of speech.

Babies do have common sounds. A study of fifteen different language environments found that babies from Africa to Scandinavia use many of the same consonants. All babies studied pronounced *m* and *b* — not much of a stretch to *Ma ma* or to *Ba ba* (Slavic for "grandmother"). And parents will have noticed too that vowel sounds are crucial building blocks for speech.[3]

So much for baby talk. We do know, however, there are some universals. While English uses a rather limited range of sounds, other languages use many, some of them totally foreign to English ears, such as the "click" sound in Xhosa (**HO-sa**) in southern Africa.

TRICONSONANTAL ROOTS

By about 1500 B.C. the priests and merchants of Ugarit had chosen twenty-nine cuneiform symbols used by their Babylonian teachers. They gave a single phonetic value to each of them. It was a true alphabet. Any word could be spelled without the cumbersome use of ideograms and syllabic signs from which many of the alphabet symbols had evolved.

To the south, Phoenicians agreed on an alphabet for writing on papyrus which had been introduced at Byblos by the Egyptians (Greek *byblos*, book). They used twenty-two signs to represent consonants. Vowels were not written. This alphabet was the source of the Greek, Etruscan, Roman, Aramaic, and South Arabian scripts and their modern European, Hebrew, Arabic, and Indic descendants.

In Semitic languages like Phoenician, words are built up from "triconsonantal" roots (composed of three consonants; **TRY-kawn-sun-ANT-il**). Vowel changes only conveyed grammatical differences like tense and case. So, for practical situations where context was clearly known, meanings were conveyed by consonants only. Vowel sounds were ignored.

Reading and writing had been simplified by the elimination of ideograms. Literacy spread. No longer mastered only by the priestly class, the system was diffused by merchants and popularized during the iron age.

ISOLATES, SETS, AND PATTERNS

In verbal communication (written and oral/aural), sounds are **isolates** (syllables), words are **sets**, and phrases, clauses, and sentences are **patterns**.

Phonemes are sounds (isolates or syllables). **Morphemes** are words or combinations of sounds (sets). **Syntax** is patterns (phrases, clauses, sentences).

You Can Say That Again!

The English sound-signal system uses:

I i   E e eu   A a aw   O oo u

plus the following sounds:

closure	air/ closure	plosive/ tongue	plosive/ lips	air/plosive/ tongue	air/plosive/ lips
L					
M			B		P
TH	TH				
N		D		T	
Z	S				
R					
J-G	SH	J			
V					F
W				(glottal)	(plosion)
	H			G	K

Read through the lists aloud and become aware of the way you make each of the sounds. Good diction is a matter of making the sound correctly so we don't end up saying F for TH in the word *with*, for instance. We don't want to confuse D and T or the listener might have some trouble.

Grimm's Law

Grimm's law explains how consonant sounds have changed in Germanic languages. Grimm's Law divides consonant sounds into **gutturals**, **dentals**, and **labials**. "Guttural" alludes to the throat, "dental" to the teeth, and "labial" to the lips.

Gutturals include **g, k, kh**, (Latin **h**) and **g**. **Dentals** include **d, t**, and **th**. **Labials** include **b, p, ph**, and **f**.

The theory explains that each Teutonic word begins one letter in its scale above the corresponding classical word. So we see the following words, beginning with some **gutturals**:

> genus — kin,
> gelid — cold,
> host — guest.

Dentals:

> dual — two,
> dactyl — toe,
> trivial — three,
> theme — doom.

Labials:

> paternal — fatherly,
> putrid — foul,
> fertile — bear,
> fragile — break.

These are simply examples showing how words may change a bit as they pass from language to language. The evolutionary path is sometimes easy to trace. At other times it can be difficult to see the relationship between words of similar origins because the words may have changed a great deal over time and as they travelled to different parts of the world, but the word *three* is found in one form or another in England, France (*trois*), Italy, and even in eastern Europe and beyond. Habits of speech make for the different spellings.

A Georgia State Language Research Centre study of bonobo apes has challenged the conventional view that language is the method of expression that distinguishes humans from other animals. They found that bonobos can communicate with words and sentences using a lexigram board of two hundred brightly coloured symbols and words. While bonobos don't have vocal cords, they can express ideas as well as a three-year-old child. Bonobos are the closest living relative to *homo sapiens* with 99 percent of a human DNA. A key factor for an individual bonobo is growing up in a language-rich environment. The research suggests new ways to teach mentally impaired and austistic children. And it suggests we might think again about the communication abilities of animals. (See Savage-Rumbaugh [1998] in the Bibliography.)

Languages are an attempt to record and convey sounds. Small deviations may become big differences once the words have been written in different languages.

WE ARE WHAT WE SPEAK

When we speak, we review the history of our culture. Words reveal where our people have been, their migration routes, and whom they met along the way. The biblical story of Esther is Hebrew with Persian roots. Biblical scholars have pointed to the similarity of Esther and

Ishtar, the Persian fertility goddess, and to the connection of Mordechai to the Iranian deity Marduk. Apparently the Jews in exile in Babylonia were influenced by Babylonian culture. Some important prayers in the Jewish liturgy are not in Hebrew but in Aramaic, because that was the language of the street two thousand and more years ago.[4]

We find Roman and Nordic gods in the names of the days of the week. In Christianity we find forms and observances reminiscent of pre-Christian practices. In English we find Latin words, some taking us back to Caesar's invasion, some to Hadrian's wall, and some entering English via French. Traces of Celtic are common. French words abound, especially after William the Conqueror. Teutonic origins are part of the mix too. And words used every day can be tracked to eastern Europe near the Danube, to a time lost in the mists of prehistory.

In North America, French, Spanish, and aboriginal languages show up in everyday English along with words brought across the Atlantic from Africa in slave ships. In Russia and Japan today, English influences are common in words and phrases adopted to deal with popular culture and the world of computers. In Japan, as in France, the "corruption" of the language by English (read American) influence is not always accepted with sanguinity (see French for "blood"). But, however we may react to foreign influences at the time of their intrusion, language cannot live in a hothouse, nor can it be frozen in time without the risk of atrophy and death. The best defence is to co-opt, and English has shown how to do this. It demonstrates that who we are and where we have been is part of how we speak today.

Lox, Language Origins, and the Universality of *Three*

The clue showing that our language origins are closely linked with those of other Indo-European languages can be found in a word like *lox* — as in the deli order of a bagel, cream cheese, and lox (salmon). There are lots of other clues, such as *three*, which translates as *tri, drei, drie, trois, tre, treis,* or *trys.* In Pakistani, Bengali, and Hindi it's *teen.* In the Punjab it's *tin.* All of them begin with a dental consonant. All of the languages represented are members of the Indo-European family, languages now found in Europe, the Americas, northern Asia, India, Afghanistan, Iran, Sri Lanka, and Australasia.

Sir William Jones, a British jurist who was in India around 1870, studied Sanskrit and discovered words that were very similar to their Greek and Latin equivalents. (Educated people at that time knew both of the classical languages.) He discovered that *three* in Sanskrit was *trayas,* much like the *tres* of Latin and *trias* of Greek. He said there was evidence linking Sanskrit to the Celtic and Germanic tongues as well, including English. English descends from the Anglo-Saxon of a few tribes along the

North Sea coast. Latin was once just the dialect of Latium. But research shows a common language source, now extinct. The conclusion is that Indo-European must have been spoken by some tribe or tribes somewhere in eastern Europe. There are lots of clues to the lineage of various modern languages. In Indo-European *cow* was *qwou*, *piglet* was *porko*, and *horse* was *ekwo*.

SOMETHING FISHY

The Indo-Europeans included fish in their diet, *pisk*; salmon or *laks* (*lox*).There were lots of salmon-like fish in fresh-water rivers in eastern Europe. But the dispute continues as to precisely where the Indo-Europeans lived. Did they live in the Danube basin or in the Caucasus? Did they live around the Aegean Sea or further west? It doesn't matter much except in the study of language lineage.

The earliest documented Indo-European languages are Hittite, Mycenaean, Greek, and Sanskrit. The Hittite documents in the cuneiform of Mesopotamia date from about 1500 B.C. The Greek texts in Mycenaean Linear B date from around 1400 BC. The Sanskrit documents are from much later but represent the language of northern India between 1400 and 1300 B.C. The experts figure Indo-Europeans existed as a single people much earlier, between 6000 and 5000 B.C.

The dispute about where the Indo-Europeans first lived is lively. The Kurganian theory favours southern Russia and Ukraine. The Danubian theory argues that the Indo-European expansion began in the Danube River valley. Wherever they started, the languages we speak in much of the world today (they are spoken by about half the human race) come from a single ancient source.

INDO-EUROPEAN LANGUAGES

BALTO-SLAVIC	INDO-IRANIAN	ITALIC
Polish	Sanskrit	Latin
Slovene	Persian	Umbrian (extinct)
Latvian	Kurdish	French
Macedonian	Hindi	Italian
Bulgarian	Urdu	Spanish
Russian	Gujarati	Portuguese
Serbo-Croatian	Punjabi	Provençal
Czech,	Romany,	Rumanian,
and others	and others	and others

GERMANIC	CELTIC	HELLENIC or GREEK
Gothic (extinct)	Irish Gaelic	Greek
Norwegian	Scottish Gaelic	
Swedish	Manx (extinct)	
Danish	Cornish (extinct)	
English	Breton	
German	Welsh	
Dutch		
Yiddish, and others		

ALBANIAN	ARMENIAN	ANATOLIAN
Albanian	Armenian	Hittite (extinct) and others (extinct)

PHOENICIAN — OUR ALPHABET

Man has been defined as a tool-using animal, but his most important tool, the one that distinguishes him from all other animals, is his speech.

— Bergan Evans

Our ABCs began around 1000 B.C., when the Greeks were trading with the Phoenicians (**fo-NEE-shunz**), who lived in what is now Lebanon.

The Phoenicians wrote from right to left. But when the Greeks experimented with *boustrophedon* (**bo-STRAWF-eh-dawn** [plough-like]) writing, they changed direction line by line, like someone ploughing a field, back and forth. They finally settled on left to right, so their letters were mirror images of the Phoenician originals.

GREEKS BEARING VOWELS

The Greeks had to use certain letters in different ways. The Phoenicians only wrote down consonants. The reader was left to fill in the vowel sounds. But some Greek words could only be distinguished by the vowels. So a few Phoenician letters were used to serve other phonetic purposes in the Greek alphabet. *Aleph, beth,* and *gimel* were retained and eventually became *alpha, beta, gamma.*[5]

Linear A is the name of the linear form of writing used in Crete from the eighteenth to fifteenth centuries B.C. Linear B was the writing using syllabic characters that was used at Knossos on Crete and on the Greek mainland from the fifteenth to the twelfth centuries B.C. for documents in the Mycenaean language.

ESPERANTO

Esperanto is an artificial language intended for international use. It was invented by a Russian philologist, L. L. Zamenof, in 1887. Esperanto is based on the most common words in major European languages. The name was Zamenof's pseudonym, "the hoping one."

There have been many attempts at creation of a language that would put an end to the problems brought about by the Tower of Babel. George Bernard Shaw promoted the idea of a universal language. He took great interest in linguistics and phonetics. And he shared the idealism of his contemporaries who were hoping to put an end to confusion and conflict through language reform. His version of the Pygmalion story (later the musical *My Fair Lady*) endowed Professor Higgins with a knowledge of speech so great he could identify a stranger's place of origin by listening to him talk. His challenge was to pass off a Cockney-burdened Covent Garden flower seller as a lady.

LINGGWISTIK REFORMATION

Shaw wasn't the only one to argue for a new, phonetic language to clean up all the strange spellings and pronunciations in English. He wasn't the first to try to correct the anomalies of English and he wasn't the last. And Professor Higgins wasn't the last person to be offended by what he considered uneducated gutter speech.

Jonathan Kates founded "Dhe Internasional Union for Dhe Kanadian Langweej." in 1987. He was determined to change the world with a new language called Kanadian.

Kates identified *"Estuari-english, a nu, repulsive, veri serius dejenerasion ov the english langweej,"* discoverd in 1983. *"It started,"* he said, *"in the estuarial rejion ov the Tams River and nao haz spreded akros haf ov England via television. It iz a dejenerasion tuward kaakni, and mani selebritis ov Britan are uzing it! It iz klir that Britan, and all anglofoonik kuntris, rekwair nasional pronunciasional instruktors."*

KANAJUN, EH?

The manifesto of "dhe Kanadian langweej" is the *"wurld's linggwistik unifier,"* a way to achieve *"internasional harmoni, kommerse, piis and happiness."* Kanadian is said to be *"rasional and konsistent, unified but multi-raisal and multi-kultural."* The reformers hope for *"linggwistik buuti, uniti and rasional konsistensi."*

So the invitation is to turn to phonetic spelling. *"Unless we du sumthing abaot fonetiks we are going tu luuz langwej totalli!"*

SEMANTICS, OR "WHAT EXACTLY DO YOU MEAN?"

"Oh, that's just semantics!" This remark is often heard in a dispute, as if to dismiss something said as no more than pointless disagreement over the meaning of a word or a phrase. That's what the term has come to mean for many people. But others will immediately think of semanticist and sometime university president and politician S. I. Hayakawa. He wrote *Language In Thought And Action* and other excellent books on general semantics.

This field of study is concerned with the way we think and use language. The wish to achieve precision in communication is a motive for the study of semantics.

So, while semantics is a word sometimes used as an epithet and thus an illustration of the problem of semantic dissonance, the term has a more useful meaning than the one of hollow rhetoric or unnecessary fine tuning of language. It doesn't simply mean a too-critical distinction in language use. Imprecision about what we mean gets us into a lot of communication difficulty. And often!

In Aristotelian terms, we say a thing is what it is: a dollar is a dollar, a rose is a rose, a chair is a chair. But semanticist Alfred Korzybski says no two things are identical and no one thing remains the same. Chair one is different from chair two is different from chair three, and so on.

THE WORD IS A CONCEPT ON WHICH WE AGREE

The semanticist says that what is empirically, phonetically, and logically a table may not have been made for use as a table. So, when we say *table,* we refer to the use of a supported flat surface. The word is just a symbol applied to a concept on which we agree (see *bank,* Etymology, Chapter 3).

Cultural conditioning is an important consideration in semantics. Hot words are tied to political "hot buttons," not because of inherent or precise meanings or usage, but because we develop prejudices. Sometimes euphemisms or code words suffice to echo shared passionate views. For one group, talk of immigration reform might mean pressure for a more generous, welcoming policy. For another group, immigration reform may mean advocacy of a more restrictive policy and even a racist message. We aren't always aware of the "load" carried by the vocabulary we use. Examples: *clean, dirty, management, labour, capitalist, socialist, law* and *order.* Of course, some loaded words are more subtle. A bigot can talk about reform and it's just a code for a discriminatory attitude. *The Silent*

Language, by anthropologist Edward T. Hall (1973), offers anecdotal examples of the vocabulary of culture and of culture as communication. Apart from whatever tribal burden we bring to our words, we bring our own, unique, personal load to each word we hear or see.

Anyone who works in radio will have an example of the caller who complains about something that hasn't even been said on air. It's about something "heard in the mind but not in the ear." And not all the misunderstanding is inadvertent or a matter of different perspectives. It can also result from the clever use of loaded words designed to influence or prejudice. Sometimes the clue is in the pronunciation, as when Winston Churchill called the Germans "**NARZ-eez.**" Or when U.S. Senator Joseph McCarthy, of witch-hunt notoriety, referred to the "**KAWM-in-ist**" threat in Hollywood.

So it is important to choose our words carefully. It's a good idea to be precise about definition and it's wise to "read between the lines" and examine closely what is really being said to us. The "politically incorrect" remark may be a simple matter of prejudice. Semantics isn't just a word. It's a warning and a subject worthy of study.

From Picture to Sound

The invention of a writing system that would represent things, ideas, and even sounds took millennia. It was a slow social and commercial evolution which began with agreement that certain symbols would carry particular meanings.

The symbols on the oldest baked clay tablets are mostly pictures. They are **pictograms**, simplified sketches — a sort of standardized shorthand.

Certain things didn't lend themselves to being represented by simple sketches, so a picture, of a jar for instance, might be altered by strokes to show a specific volume. Or marks on the jar might distinguish the contents, beer from barley for example. Archeologists have determined that this was already the practice in Sumeria in about 4000 B.C.

Sometimes the symbols and signs represented not things, but ideas, or even names. The system had grown from being purely **pictographic** to being **ideographic**. The Sumerians took another giant step when they decided to have some signs or pictures represent sounds such as "**ka**" which meant mouth. The symbol had evolved from a picture of a human head.

A Sound Idea

The phonetic value represented by a symbol or **phonogram** made it possible to spell out names and compound words instead of having to invent new ideograms. The Sumerian system grew into one that used a combination of pictures, signs, and phonograms.

The increasing usefulness of phonograms (modified for specificity by attached ideograms) made it possible to reduce the total number of signs in use. Soon after 3000 B.C. the total was cut from around two thousand signs to about eight hundred. By 2500 B.C. the Sumerians were using about six hundred signs. And the symbols gradually became more cursory. Eventually they evolved into cuneiform, the wedge-shaped marks made in wet clay by a stylus cut from a reed. The Sumerians also developed both decimal and sexagesimal numeric systems for accounting. Numerals were strokes, one to nine [ )))))))))] and 0, made with the circular end of the stylus, for ten.

Underlying the invention of writing to represent the spoken word was the need to manage food supply and trade. It happened when an urban civilization had developed and people agreed to co-operate. They agreed on the standard, arbitrary meanings of sounds and written symbols. Soon people speaking other languages found it useful to use the Sumerian system.

THE TOWER OF BABEL

> *Therefore is the name of it called Babel because the Lord did there confound the language of all the earth.*
>
> — Genesis

Cyrus the Great and his Persian army waited outside the walls of Babylon, hoping to starve the city into submission. It was the end of a series of campaigns in which the Persians conquered the Medes and the rich land of Lydia.

The Babylonians stockpiled food but forgot about a major defensive weakness, the Euphrates. It flowed through the centre of town. Cyrus had a canal dug from some upstream marshes and the level of the river dropped low enough for the Persian troops to be able to wade into the centre of town.

With the taking of Babylon, Cyrus reigned over Mesopotamia[6], Syria, and Palestine. According to the Greek historians Herodotus and Xenophon, Cyrus treated the Babylonians well.

The biblical prophet Daniel, however, saw the conquest as divine vengeance. He relates how Belshazzar, the regent managing state affairs for his father Nabonidus (**na-BAWN-i-dus**), was giving a feast at which the guests drank wine from the sacred vessels of the Jews.[7]

As the guests feasted, the words *Mene, Mene, Tekel, Upharsin* appeared on the walls. Daniel interpreted the message as God saying the kingdom was finished, to be divided between the Medes and the Persians.[8]

Cyrus ended the long exile of the Jews in Babylon and sent them back to rebuild Jerusalem and Solomon's temple.

Babylon was the world's largest city. Dominating the river's wharves was a huge ziggurat — the Tower of Babel mentioned in Genesis. It was an artificial mound of mud bricks ninety metres high. The Babylonians called it Etemenanki, "House of the Platform of Heaven and Earth." Across town were the famous Hanging Gardens of Babylon.

But the city's glory came to an end when Cyrus took charge. Babylon became an important part of the Persian Empire, but in 482 B.C. it revolted against Xerxes (**ZIRK-seez**). In 331 B.C. the city surrendered to Alexander the Great. Its ruins stood for more than two thousand years.[9]

And the whole earth was of one language and of one speech.... And they said to one another, Go to, let us make brick, and burn them thoroughly ... let us build us a city, and a tower, whose top may reach unto heaven.... And the Lord came down to see the city and the tower.... And the Lord said, Behold, the people is one, and they have all one language.... Go to, let us go down, and there confound their language, that they may not understand one another's speech. So the Lord scattered them abroad ... upon the face of all the earth: ... the Lord did there confound the language of all the earth.... (Genesis 11:1-9, King James Version)

NOTES

1. The rear-guard action in defence of the French language is discussed elsewhere, but it is interesting that one staunch defender, Maurice Druon, secretary of the Académie française, accused American feminists of contributing to the pollution of *la belle langue* with an insistence on politically correct usage. In *Le Figaro* Druon wrote in 1998 that from the Quebec staging post, "contaminated by geographical proximity," a trend toward feminine titles has gained support. In the Lionel Jospin cabinet, female cabinet ministers came to be known as *Madame la Ministre* instead of *Madame le Ministre*. The government also uses *directrice* instead of *directeur*. Druon laments as well that Belgians have fallen prey to "Americanomania" with the laughable term *sapeuses-pompières* (firewomen).

2. See acronyms such as *FUBAR* in Chapter 7.

3. Baby talk used by adults talking to infants isn't pointless cooing. Scientists say it seems to be vital in helping baby brains absorb key components of language. The high-pitched, drawled speech is universal. Parents exaggerate

vowel sounds for mastery of the phonetic elements of speech: "Loooook at Maawmmy's pretty beeeeds." A study by Patricia Kuhl of the University of Washington found that five-month-old children begin to enunciate the three vowel sounds common to all languages. They are **ee, ah,** and **oo.** Kuhl's work in 1992 found that six-month-old children learned to categorize meaningful vowel sounds while ignoring subtle distinctions of little use to them. Kuhl found that certain sounds attract babies. They turn to adults who use singsong baby talk. International research found that in Swedish, Russian, and English, mothers commonly exaggerate the important vowels, the **ee, ah,** and **oo** sounds important to babies learning language.

Other research shows that infants, as young as eight months, are listening, hearing, and remembering words. Reading to children in these early months helps them make a start with the language-learning process. They learn about sounds and patterns. Tape-recorded stories were played to eight-month-old children once a day over ten days. Two weeks later the infants were more attentive to lists of words they knew from the stories they had heard. It may explain the vocabulary spurt at eighteen to twenty-one months of age, when children use more and more words. One possible reason is that the child has remembered a number of words and at eighteen months the child associates the labels with objects.

4. *Eloi, Eloi, lama sabachthani?* (My God, my God, why hast thou forsaken me?) According to Matthew this was Jesus' last cry; it was in Aramaic. Twenty-five hundred years ago this language spread from Pakistan to southern Egypt. While Jesus may have known Hebrew and some Greek, Aramaic was almost certainly the tongue of Galilee. It is the source of the modern Hebrew alphabet.

5. Compare alphabets — Hebrew, Arabic, Greek, Russian, and Sanskrit — in *Webster's New Collegiate Dictionary.*

6. Mesopotamia means "between two rivers" (Tigris and Euphrates).

7. The Babylonians under Nebuchadnezzar II (**NEB-oo-kad-NEZ-ar**) had stolen them from Jerusalem forty-seven years earlier.

8. One man's Mede is another man's Persian. See Puns in Chapter 3.

9. Until 1990, when Iraq's Saddam Hussein bulldozed most of them so foundations could be laid for what he called a "New Babylon."

Quiz 3
?

1) What is an **isolate**? What is a **set**? Give an example of each. _____
   _____

2) Explain the **yo-he-ho** theory of speech origin. _____
   _____

3) What did *boustrophedon* mean in early writing? Which syllable gets the main emphasis? _____

4) In Indo-European, what was the word for *horse*? _____
   For *fish*? _____

5) *Mesopotamia* means _____

For answers, see Appendix A.

CHAPTER THREE

Word Origins

CHAPTER THREE

Word Origins

Etymology, slang, jargon, euphemisms, spoonerisms, bowdlerism, puns, limericks, swearing, and the origin of "30"

When the mind is thinking, it is talking to itself.
— Plato

We often wonder where a word comes from or why it is pronounced as it is when phonetic logic dictates otherwise. Word origins illustrate how much fun it is to inquire. Certain word origins surprise us. For example, the verb *to testify* has the same root as *testicle*. Someone who dies *intestate* is someone who didn't make a will. Sometimes we find a modern usage has nothing to do with the word's origins. Sometimes we find a core pronunciation preserved over time. But often pronunciation has been altered over the years (see **testify**, Word Origins, this chapter). And, speaking of gonads, is it possible that the Spanish word *cojones* (**ko-HO-nayz**) will take on the meaning of courage in everyday English as it has now in slang?

> Q. (**in court**): "Answer the question. When did they have a knife
>   at your throat?"
> A.: "That was a figure of speech."
> Q.: "So they had a figure of speech at your throat?"

This book is not an etymological dictionary. Far from it. But it does present a few words along with their origins in order to illustrate how digging into the history of a word can enhance our understanding. We will follow the evolution of certain words, current spelling, pronunciation, and usage. By the way, *entomology* deals with insects.

Many words come to us via slang. Sometimes the words were invented. They also may have been appropriated for particular purposes, usually by people who shared a special group perspective. They may have come from an industry, a craft, or from the arts. *Jazz* is a case in point; jazz slang has been appropriated by other arts. An *axe* came to mean a musician's instrument, such as a cornet or saxophone. Soon it came to mean almost any musical instrument. *Cool*, *hot*, and the word *jazz* itself, are all words from the vocabulary of Black American music. But they have all found broader usage.

THE F-WORD

Euphemisms are a way to avoid the use of certain words and phrases. Sometimes we resort to a euphemism in order to deal with a distasteful topic. At other times we choose our words carefully so as to avoid giving offence, to sidestep a taboo. *Making love* is used to mean "copulation." Copulation is a technical term for sexual intercourse. The F-word, so often heard in common, everyday speech and occasionally used as a word-by-word punctuation, also means to copulate. It is considered obscene, but it simply means to copulate. In Atlantic Canada they talk or sing about *friggin' in the riggin'*, using a word that approximates the one so often used as an expletive but still found to be beyond the pale in polite company. *Frig* is from Latin *fricare* — to masturbate. Pierre Trudeau once insisted he said in the House of Commons, "Fuddle duddle," when he was actually heard saying to another honourable member, "F—-off!" In *The Naked and the Dead*, Norman Mailer used the word *fug*. That led to the joke that Mailer was such a lousy writer he couldn't even spell the F-word. The word has Indo-European roots of course. Why else would we find *fokken* in Middle Dutch, *focka* in Swedish (meaning "to copulate") and *fuken* in German? While on this topic, it is interesting to note that the term *intercourse*, in some situations now, is no longer used to signify social contact, because it is so often employed to mean sexual congress. *Schmuck*, on the other hand, still means "penis" in Yiddish.

One doesn't often see vulgar words in print. Perhaps in novels. But one certainly hears them in movies and more and more often on television. Natural dialogue helps establish credibility. The trouble is, too often the street language used is gratuitously shocking. It isn't employed because it helps us understand a character or a situation. It has dramatic value simply because it shocks. It serves the same function in humour. As discussed elsewhere in this book, we have different standards for different situations. We do have standards, though, as long as we don't argue for the lowest common denominator at all times.

In the list of troublesome words in Chapter 5 you will find some F-words with different meanings but with sounds that come close to the offensive term. The F-word itself probably comes from Norwegian or Swedish. One dictionary states it is often used as a "meaningless intensive." And that is one way in which a word can lose its usefulness but still maintain its taboo offensiveness.

CRAPPER

Sometimes a circumlocution is innocent. At other times it is used to soften impact or conceal a hidden agenda. Occasionally a euphemism succeeds so well we can no longer use it. For instance, the word for Sir Thomas Crapper's device, the toilet, can no longer be used as a short form for the bodily function in polite company. Ladies will "powder their noses." A brief history of "bowdlerisms" is recounted in this chapter with an introduction to Bowdler and his dedicated sister. And we will also take a look at the cultural peculiarities of swearing. A taboo for one group is innocent for another. No offence intended.

PROFESSOR SPOONER

Spoonerisms are fun. But they can be embarrassing. When a radio announcer wants to say, "the best in bread," and says instead, "the breast in bed," we laugh at the broadcaster's expense. Spoonerisms are simply the transposition of letters, sounds, or syllables. Sometimes they are caused by stress, at other times by inattention, and they are usually completely innocent as well as harmless. Spoonerisms may be a form of dyslexia. They turn up in puns, intentional and unintentional. Most of the time we want to avoid them, unless we intend to prompt a chuckle.

GROANERS

Puns, on the other hand, are "the lowest form of humour," in which we all delight. Certain puns are based on the use of a word that sounds like another word with a different meaning. Other puns are just overextended metaphors. And everyone likes to join the fun when a group extends a pun to its most ridiculous extremes:

> "There's something *fishy* going on." "Agreed! And thereby hangs a *tail*." "Right! And I am fed up to the *gills*!" "Agreed! This is confusion on a grand *scale*." "They think we'll go for it '*hook, line, and sinker*.'" "Well, I'm from a different *school*. This whole project will go *belly up*." "Relax *old trout*, stop *floundering* around."

The more pained the groan in response, the happier the punster. Later in this chapter we'll offer more examples — just for the *pun* of it.

One malapropism that became part of the everyday repertoire was the confusion between *condom* and *condo* (short for *condominium*). Another turned up in a shampoo commercial. In one version of it a woman on an airliner shouts with joy. In another version a young woman is audibly thrilled in a supermarket. In each case the word *organic* is purposely confused with *orgasmic*. Dr. Ruth, the famed pop sexologist, turns up with her grocery cart to suggest, in English with a heavy German accent, "If you think that's great, try the body wash!" For more examples, check **Spoonerisms** in the list below and **Science**

Bloopers in Chapter 5. And worth remembering, perhaps, is the reference to the president's office in the White House during the Clinton administration as the *Oral Office*.

The great vaudeville and radio comedian Fred Allen said about punsters, "Hanging is too good for them. They should be drawn and quoted!"

POCKET POESY

Limericks can be nonsense, as in the case of Edward Lear. Limericks can be pointed and pornographic. Limericks are comic classics. Limericks are a bit like puns in that they tempt us to join the fun by trying our hand at their creation. "There was an old man of Siam, who . . . (fill in the blanks) . . . that indignant old man of Siam." There are whole books of limericks. This chapter offers just a few examples.

SOME WORD ORIGINS

The prime purpose of this potpourri (**PO-poor-EE**) chapter is to provide a brief list of word origins. If words are fun, one of the most entertaining things about them is how they evolved from their sometimes mysterious origins:

Abracadabra can be traced back to a mythical Persian sun god. The letters add up — in numerology — to 365. The word is not a corruption of the cabbalistic *habraha dabar* (Hebrew for "bless the object").

Accent — from the Latin *ad* + *cantus*, representing the Greek *prosoidia* (prosody). Syllables spoken with a **grave** (**GRAV**) **accent** (`) were in deep voice. **Acute** (´) **accent** words were spoken a musical fifth higher. Those with a **circumflex** (^) began high and dropped a fifth. With the shift from length and pitch to volume, the word *accent* came to mean the stress or a sign indicating emphasis.

Alderman comes from Anglo-Saxon *ealdorman*, parent or head of family. The word persists in a political context due to the fact that many of the forms of social organization of Anglo-Saxon England were retained even after William the Conqueror's restructuring of the island. *Sheriff is* another example. A sheriff is an important shire or county official with judicial responsibilities. See **ward**.

Algebra is derived from Arabic *al* + *jebr*, reunion of broken parts. The concept of zero came to western Europe via the Arabs. In science there are a number of terms of Arab origin.

Assassin is from the Arabic *hash shashin* (hashish[1] eaters), an organized secret society in Persia in the eleventh century. Existentialist philosopher Jean Paul Sartre and fellow writer Simone de Beauvoir spent much of their leisure time in a Montparnasse (Paris) boîte called *Aux assassins*.

Bafflegab is a word invented in about 1952 by Milton Smith, the assistant general counsel for the U.S. Chamber of Commerce. It was a contest entry and it won. Its definition: "multiloquence characterized by a consummate interfusion of circomlocution ... and other familiar manifestations of abstruse expiation commonly utilized for promulgations implementing procrustean determinations by government bodies." It means, in short, bureaucratic B.S.

Bank in both Anglo-Saxon and Latin originally meant something flat like a shelf. At some point it came to mean "bench." Lombard money managers used to sit on a bench.

Barbarous finds its roots in Latin and Greek, meaning "foreign," "ignorant," "uncivilized." (And a bluebeard [*barbe bleue*] is a man who murders his wives.)

Bedfordshire — To go to Bedfordshire means "to retire for the night."

Bible comes from Byblos, the ancient Phoenician city from which papyrus was exported. It came to mean "book" and then "sacred scriptures, invested with a supernatural power." The Bible and the Word are considered (by fundamentalists) the work of God, not men.

Blooper — an embarrassing blunder, usually a vocal one. The term is also used in baseball to signify a looping pitch or a ball hit high just beyond the infielders. In broadcasting there are collections of bloopers, recordings of on-air gaffes including spoonerisms. The author recalls a moment on the CBC's "World At Six" when a late-breaking story out of Chicago told of a company picnic which ended with hundreds of picnickers suffering food poisoning. It was a serious item. This was no time for levity. I read the copy cold and referred to the "hundreds of ill **PICK-i-NIK-urz**." I quickly corrected myself and said emphatically, "Of course that should read **PIK-nurz**!" Wrong twice in a row, I moved on. Another type of blooper involves the difference between the way we see some symbols and the way we hear or say them. On a final edition of the same "World At Six" broadcast to the West Coast and the Yukon, a story was rushed in about a labour dispute at Vancouver Harbour. The story mentioned the head of the harbour administration and identified him as B. D. I. Johnson. No problem when you read the initials silently. But read them aloud, as I did, and suddenly you are describing Johnson as "beady-eyed." Not at all complimentary. To make things worse, a giggle threatened, and my co-anchor took over the tail lights (reprise of top-story headlines). My sign-off and network cue were a bit breathless.

Blurb is the name given to the dust-jacket prose that describes a book. A blurb can also be a public-relations release or a short promotional paragraph on a person or event. *Webster* defines it as: "a laudatory advertisement, especially for a book." *Blurb* was invented by humorist Gelett Burgess in 1907 on a dust jacket added to his book *"Are You A Bromide?"* His publisher later said that it was common practice to print the picture of a damsel — languishing, heroic, coquettish — on the jacket of a novel. So Burgess lifted from a Lydia Pinkham or tooth-powder advertisement the portrait of a sweet young woman, then painted in some gleaming teeth, enhanced the damsel's appearance, and put her in the centre of the dust jacket. His accompanying text was nonsense about Miss Belinda Blurb.

Boondoggle was originally an American word for "gadget." When the New York Board of Estimates investigated the use of relief money in 1935, it was said an artist's project produced leather crafts, three-ply carving, and boondoggles. It has come to mean "spending time doing nothing."

Bourgeois originally meant "citizen," somebody who lived in a city or town as distinguished from a nobleman or a serf. Thus, middle class. Now it usually means middle class or capitalist. It is sometimes used to designate unsophisticated people. In Canada, the French word meant historically "a trader and leader in the fur trade" and was anglicized by trappers and mountainmen to *bushwa* meaning "nonsense."

Bowdlerize — The term means "to delete expressions considered offensive or to alter them." Dr. Thomas Bowdler took his scalpel to the bard and gave his name to a practice much more offensive than the Shakespearean language he found objectionable. See **Bowdlerize** later in this chapter.

Boycott — Captain Boycott was an agent for an Irish landlord. In 1880 the Irish Land League gave him the treatment now associated with his name.

Brodie, Steve — "... do a Brodie." He jumped from the Brooklyn Bridge and was unharmed.

Calculate is derived from the Latin word for pebble. Pebbles were used for counting.

Christian is from the Latin *chrisma* (oil for anointing). Christ is the Anointed One (see **Xmas**).

Church — The Greeks had a word for it, three in fact. One, *ekklesia*, for the general assembly in Athens, became the French *église*. *Basilike* became *basilica*. And *kuriakon* is from *kurios* for "lord." In a long journey across Europe, *kuriakon* became Scottish *kirk* and English *church*.

Court — In Old French it meant a poultry yard, but it came to mean the territory of the king and later the area where he dispensed justice. A woman of the court was a *courtesan,* but behaviour changed the meaning of the word.

Courtesy is behaviour that would grace a court.

Coventry — "To be sent to Coventry" is to be sent into seclusion, to be banished. *Covent,* as in *Covent Garden,* really means "convent." There was once a convent in London near the modern Covent Garden. The word *convent* is related to the word *convene,* meaning "to meet." But "being sent to Coventry" means "to be put out of touch." The British city in the West Midlands is the place where Lady Godiva rode horseback clothed only in her chastity. She did it to persuade her husband Earl Leofric, to cancel a heavy tax in Mercia.

Curfew is from the French *couvre-feu* (cover fire).

Daffodil — *Asphodel* was the name of a Greek flower. Latin *affodillus* became the English *affodil* which became *daffodil.*

Date — In ancient Rome, letters began *Data Romae* meaning "given at Rome" (followed by the date). In English *date* came to mean the time rather than "given." On the other hand, the Greek word for finger gives us the other *date. Daktylos,* finger, indicates the shape of the fruit of the palm. But it could be that the origin of the word is actually from the Arabic *daqal* for "palm."

Debunk — A Latin prefix was added to the American word *buncombe,* yielding *de + bunk.* The term came out of the debates on the Missouri Compromise. Felix Walker, the member for Buncombe County, North Carolina, refused to stop for a vote. He said he wasn't talking to the House but to his constituents in Buncombe. (For more political names and terms, see Chapter 5.)

Demijohn — This is not half a John but a corruption of the French *dame Jeanne* which means Lady Jane. It is used in Italian and Spanish, too. It could be a distortion of Damaghan, the Persian town where glass was blown. It's just one of the many words used by sailors to refer to either drink or containers.

Derrick — First used to refer to persons, the word comes from the name of the hangman at Tyburn prison, Derrick. Eventually the name was transferred to the instrument and came to be applied to any machine used for hoisting.

Devil — Slander is a great evil and, in Old English, *deofol* — from the Greek *diabolos* — meant "slanderer."

Eureka — The ancient king Hiero wanted to know if the golden crown he'd been given was made of real gold. While Archimedes was taking a bath it occurred to him that a body must displace its own weight in water — this was a way to test the crown. "*Eureka!*" he shouted. It's from the Greek verb *heuriskein* (to find). The logical art of discovery is *heuretic* and the modern art of education is *heuristic.* Pupils are taught to find out things on their own. If they do, it's called scholarship.

Europe — The Assyrians called the land of the rising sun *Asu* and the land of the setting sun *Ereb.* The Greeks picked up the terms for Asia and Europe. Later came the legend of Europa, daughter of Phoenix, carried off by Zeus in the disguise of a bull. She was to become the mother of Minos, related to the Minotaur or "bull of Minos" (Latin *taurus*). The Minotaur lurked in the Labyrinth. Theseus (**THEES-yus**) slew the Minotaur ... and so on.

Fan — From *fanatic* from the Latin *fanum*, an overwrought religious person found around a temple.

Fascist — Roman builders carried their axe in a bundle of rods. The Latin for "band," *fascia*, gave the name to the bundles which became a symbol of authority for local Roman magistrates. We find the root in the English word *fascinate.* The bundle-and-axe symbol was adopted by Benito Mussolini's Fascist Party. The symbol was in the rondel on the Italian aircraft that flew for the Fascists in the Spanish Civil War.

Fifth Column — This term originated in the Spanish Civil War when one of dictator Franco's generals said he had four columns of troops advancing on Madrid and a fifth inside its walls (spies, informers).

Gladstone — a small bag, portmanteau, also a claret which became more available after Gladstone reduced a tariff on imported wine in 1860.

Halloween — This is short for *All Hallows Eve. Hallow* can be traced back through Middle to Old English and means "holy" or "respected greatly." *Ween* is from *even* which means "evening." The October 31st events can be traced back to pagan rituals. The feast has been observed on that date since the eighth century. It was chosen to honour Christian saints and martyrs. Ancient Celts believed it was the date when the recently deceased chose bodies of people or animals to inhabit for the next year. To frighten the spirits away, the Celts dressed as demons, hobgoblins, and witches.

Harangue — The German initial *h* or *ch* was hard for speakers of Romance languages to say before another consonant, so it was often dropped, as in the word *hring* which meant "people sitting around (the king) in a circle." *Ring* and *rank* have the same origins. *Harangue* came to mean "the noise made by people sitting in a ring around the king."

Hobson's Choice — Thomas Hobson, a seventeenth-century London stableman, made everyone hiring a horse take the next one in order.

Homage — (**HAW-mij** or **AW-mij**, NOT **o-MAWZH!**). It comes from Old French, where the word was a derivative from the Latin *homo*, meaning "man." In the feudal scheme of things it meant the "fealty of a vassal." Literally "to worship" or "pay respect to" is the common meaning. But a new pronunciation seems to have come to us from the Hollywood film industry, where they think it is clever to say certain things with a French accent. It may be **o-MAWZH** in French, but the correct English pronunciation is **HAW-mij**.

Infantry — The word comes from the Latin *in* (for "not"), *fans* (for "speaking," from *fari*, "to speak"). It became *infanteria*, meaning "those unqualified for the cavalry."

Insemination, artificial — The root is *seminal*, for "seed" or "semen." A seminary is a nursery, where something originates. To inseminate is to sow. To artificially inseminate is to implant preserved semen in a female in order to fertilize an ovum. The word is pronounced "**in-SEM-in-AY-shun**," NOT "**in-sem-NAY-shun**." *In vitro* simply means "in glass," "in a test tube."

Jargon — The French word *argot* (**ar-GO**) can be traced to the Italian *gargo* or to the Latin *argutari* meaning "to dispute." *Argutus* means "tricky." *Lingua gerga* is sacred language only known by the initiated.

Jazz is an African word which may have meant "hurry." Or is it perhaps the name of a man in Vicksburg who gained fame in 1910 for asking everyone to, "Come on an' hear Alexander's Ragtime Band"? Alexander's first name was Charles, Chas. for short and said, "Chazz!" Or perhaps *jazz* is from:

> *Jazib* (Arab) — one who allures,
> *Jazba* (Hindu) — ardent desire, or
> *Jaiza* (African) — rumble of distant drums.

Another theory suggests that the word originated in the brothels of New Orleans, where it meant, simply, "sexual intercourse."

Jeopardy is an excellent name for a television game show based on knowledge of trivia and hosted smoothly by Canadian Alex Trebek who once performed for the CBC in Toronto and Ottawa. The multilingual Trebek offers flawless pronunciation over a broad range of subjects and languages. When a game was played to a draw, the Romans called it *jocus partitus*. In French it became *jeu parti*. Later it came to mean an unknown result or uncertainty.

Kangaroo is a word invented by Captain Cook and probably a corruption of the native words for "don't understand."

Ketchup or **Catsup** comes from the Malay *kechap* or perhaps from the Japanese *kitjap* meaning "sauce."

Laconic — Spartans had little to say or spoke with economy and, since Sparta was the city-state capital of Laconia, the use of this term became a way of describing those who were not very talkative (Greek *lakon*). *Spartan* means "frugal" or "stern" or "austere."

Lady — see **Ward**.

Lieutenant is pronounced "lef-TEN-ant." It may be **LOO-ten-ant** in the United States and that may seem closer to the French, but the English and Canadian pronunciation has been around a long time, six centuries in fact. The word comes from *leuf*, one of the Old French spellings of *lieu*. It may have resulted from a confusion between the letters *v* and *u*. The spelling was *lievtenant* or *lufftenant* or *lefftenant*. In the fourteenth century there was no standardized spelling. When printing presses, however, started to mass-produce books in the fifteenth century, more attention was paid to spelling and standards began to develop. The word *lieutenant* comes from *lieu*, as shown above, which means "place" and *tenant*, which means "to hold." *Tenant* has the same root as the French verb *tenir* (to hold). A lieutenant is someone who takes the place of another, someone who stands in to exercise the authority of someone else. So, while there can be no question as to the word's French roots, the pronunciation **lef-TEN-ant** has history on its side.

Macaroni comes from the Italian *maccheroni* which signifies a mixture of meal, eggs, and so on. In the late 1700s some English fops formed the Macaroni Club dedicated to the rejection of native food. Hence came *"Yankee Doodle Dandy, riding on his pony and eating macaroni..."* See also **Yankee**.

Malapropism — We owe this term to Mrs. Malaprop in Sheridan's play *The Rivals* (1775). It signifies the mistaken use of a word that sounds a bit like another (*condom* and *condominium*).

Maverick comes from Samuel Maverick, a Texan who pastured his cattle on an island. His name came to mean "unbranded calves" and eventually "politicians who wore no party label."

Mentor — the teacher of Telemachus in the *Odyssey*.

Melba Toast was named after opera singer Nellie Melba (Helen Porter Mitchell of Australia, 1861-1931). *Melba* derives from Melbourne, Australia. Also named after the opera singer was the dish Peach Melba.

Morphine — a narcotic named after Morpheus, the Roman god of sleep.

Nest probably comes to us all the way from Sanskrit. In Latin it's *nidus* as in the scientific term *nidification* for "nest building." The Sanskrit word was *nidd*, from *nizd* which was a combination of *ni* (down) and *sed* (to sit). A nest egg was an egg (real or artificial) left in the nest to encourage the laying of more.

Nicotine was named after Jacques Nicot who in 1560 introduced tobacco to France. In fact, the whole *nicotiana* plant species is named after him (see **Eponym** in Chapter 7). *Tobacco*, on the other hand, comes from Spanish *tabaco*, for the large tube which the Spanish saw the Indians smoking.

Nomad — member of a roaming tribe, from Greek *nomas* (pasture).

Numnah — pronounced **NUM-na**, saddle cloth or pad for under saddle, from Hindi *namda* from Persian *namad* (carpet).

Obliterate means "to wipe off letters." It is a combination of the Latin *ob* (off) and *litera* (letter) which actually comes from *linere* (to smear, as on parchment). *Literal, literature, literate,* and *letters* all come from this source.

Occam's Razor — the principle that no more assumptions should be made than are necessary when examining or analyzing a thing. This principle of parsimony is attributed to William of Occam (**O-KAM**), the fourteenth-century English philosopher.

Odyssey originally signified the journey of Odysseus (**o-DEES-yus**) as described by Homer.

Ouija Board — the board that can't say no in either French or German.

Pandemonium — the capital of hell in Milton's *Paradise Lost*.

Philippics — name given to Demosthenes' (**dem-AWS-than-eez**) orations against Philip of Macedon (**MASS-eh-dawn**).

Plagiarism comes from the Latin for "kidnapping," from *plaga* (a net). Milton said borrowing without improving is "a plagerie."

Pornography — from Greek *porne* (harlot) and *graphos* (writing).

Procrustean we owe to the Greek giant Procrustes (**pro-KRUS-teez**). The term means "forcing conformity."

Quarantine — from popular Latin *quaranta* derived from classical Latin *quadraginta* (forty). At first it applied to the forty days of Lent. Then it was applied to the forty days a widow could stay in her late husband's home before she had to give it up to the heir. Later it was used to signify the forty-day period during which a ship from an infected port had to wait before landing.

Quisling — This term for a betrayer came from the name of the head of the Norwegian Nazi Party after the Germans invaded in 1940. Major Vidkum Quisling is universally remembered for betrayal. For Americans, General Benedict Arnold has a similar standing. At one point he tried to capture Quebec. He failed. Later, in 1780, he betrayed the American revolution.

Quixotic (**kwix-AW-tik**) originated with Cervantes (**sir-VAN-tayz**) who wrote about Don Quixote (**kee-HO-tay**), the Man from La Mancha, an idealistic knight who tilted at windmills with aid from sidekick Sancho Panza. Spanish *quixote* comes from *quijote*, from the Latin *coxa* (hip). The English equivalent is *cuisse* (from old French) for "thigh armour."

Rap is the sound of a knock on the door. But if you don't give a rap, it means that you wouldn't pay a *rap* which was a counterfeit Irish coin of the eighteenth century. Now *rap* means "the rhythmic inner-city chanting of rappers." Some have taken anti-police anger and the frustration of the ghetto to creative heights and to multi-million-dollar rewards.

Riding is a common English word of Germanic origin. The Romans divided towns into quarters, so today Paris is divided into *quartiers*. But the English divided the countryside into thirds (Old English *thrithing* from Old Norse). *Norththrithing* became *Northriding*. Eventually the *North* and *Sud* were dropped, leaving *riding*. Now it is the term for a constituency in parliamentary elections. *North* and *Sud*, from French, still turn up in place names such as Northumberland or Sudbury.

Rostrum — This word for a speaker's platform comes from the Latin for "beak." The prows of ships were extended with decorative beaks and the platform in the Roman forum was similarly decorated.

Sadist — This term originated with the Comte de Sade (1740–1814), who is said to have lived a life of excess and to have enjoyed inflicting pain. *Masochist* originated with Leopold Von Sacher-Masoch (1835–95) and refers to those who enjoy pain. These terms are **eponyms** (see Chapter 7). *Lechery* is not; it probably comes from old French *lecheur*, from Frankish meaning "lick." *Chacun à son goût*, as they say.

Sandwich — John Montague (**MAWN-ti-gyoo**), the earl of Sandwich who died in 1792, was a great gambler who would not leave the gaming table to eat. He was once brought beef between slices of bread. Obviously it had been done before, but his name stuck to the idea. This is another eponym.

Saxophone — named after Antoine J. Sax.

Schedule — (**SHEJ-ul**, Canadian; **SHED-yool**, British; and **SKEJ-ul**, American) — The term comes from Latin *schedula* via French. It, in turn, derived from the Greek *skhede* (papyrus leaf). At first it signified a written document, later an inventory, a timetable, or an agenda.

Word Origins

Sequoia (seh-KWOY-a) — a California conifer, named after the man who invented the Cherokee syllabary.

Slang is derived from the Dutch for "snake." It was used to signify the chains on prisoners and later for the talk of criminals. See the section on slang in this chapter.

Spartan — see **Laconic**.

Spoonerisms — Some people, when excited or embarrassed, transpose the first letters of words as did the Reverend W. A. Spooner: *"Mardon me, Padam, this pie is occupued."* There is also a story of a woman who wrote a book about her husband's fatal heart attack. Three years later she did an interview which fell apart in giggles when she opened with *"My husband had his hatal fart attack ..."* And then there was the clergyman who introduced the British blonde starlet Diana (née Fluck) Dors as *"... soon to be a star ... Miss Diana Clunt...."* The phrase weather forecasters don't use when referring to twisters is *"sucking funnel of wind"*!

Sybaritic (SIB-ar-IT-ik) comes from the name of a town in southern Italy known for its luxurious ways. The city was mentioned by Plutarch in his description of the Parthian victory train and all the concubines it contained after the defeat of Crassus.

Testify — The word comes from *testes*. A gesture takes on legal import, "I swear," with a hand held protectively over the genitals.

Thug is derived from the Hindi *thaga* which means "to deceive." In India, thuggery was organized crime until the British suppressed it in 1830. Thugs usually deceived a victim until they were in a position to strangle him.

Tongue — We sometimes say *tongue* to mean "language." *Language* is derived from *langue*, which is French for "tongue" from the Latin *lingua*. So we get *lingua franca*, a language used around the world. Today that tongue is English.

Tuxedo comes from the Algonkian word *p'tuksit* (**TOOK-sit**), meaning "round-footed" or "wolflike," as were the members of the Wolf Tribe of the Delaware Indians in New York State. Tuxedo Lake and Tuxedo Park were named after them. Tuxedo Park became a luxury resort when taken over by the Lorillard family. And Griswold Lorillard first wore the tailless dinner jacket which came to be called a **tuxedo**.

Ubiquitous comes from the Latin *ubique*, which means "everywhere."

Umbrage — This is probably the most entertaining and oft-told word-origin story: Alexander the Great stands before Diogenes who is dressed in a barrel and carrying a lamp in the daylight as he looks for an honest man. Alexander tells Diogenes he may have anything he wants. Diogenes takes *umbrage*. He asks Alexander to step out of his light. *Umbra* means "shadow."

Venal — A venal person is one who can be bought. It comes from the Latin *venum* which means "goods for sale." (French *vendre*; a *vendu* is a sellout.)

Venial is not the same as **venal**. It comes from the Latin *venialis*, the adjectival form of *venia*, pardon.

Veto — A Roman tribune was given the power in the name of the people to cancel certain bills of the Senate or edicts from magistrates. He did so by saying simply, "Veto" (I forbid). *Vetare* is the infinitive for the Latin verb meaning "to forbid."

Volcano — from Vulcan, the blacksmith of the Roman gods, husband of Venus.

Ward comes from the Old English *weard*. The lord was the *hlafweard* (in charge of the bread). His wife was the *hlaefdige*: *hlaf* (loaf) + *dig* (to knead). *Hlaefdige* became *lady*.

Wart comes from Old English *wearte* (skin) to mean "a horny projection on the skin (caused by a virus)."

Week — In Anglo-Saxon this was the word for service. Sunday is the day of the sun, Monday the day of the moon, Tuesday the day of Tiw, the Teutonic god of war. Mars is the Roman god of war. Thus the French *mardi* for "Tuesday." Wednesday is Woden's day (Norse). Thursday is Thor's day. Friday is for Friya, the Norse goddess of love and wife of Woden. Saturday is the day of Saturn, the Roman god of agriculture.

Whiskey — from Scottish Gaelic *usquebaugh*, meaning "water of life."

Word — *"In the beginning was the word."* The term comes from Sanskrit *vratum* which meant "command" or "law." In Latin it is *verbum* which evolved through Teutonic (Germanic) forms to *word*.

Wort — from Old English *wyrt*, meaning "root," "herb," or "plant." The term turns up in plant names like St. John's Wort. It is also used in brewing, where it signifies a diluted solution of sugars from malt. When fermented this solution becomes beer. See **Zythepsary**.

Xanthippe (zan-THIP-ee), shrewish wife of Socrates. Thus, "She is a regular Xanthippe...."

Xenogamy (zen-AWG-a-me) — the custom of a tribe to allow marriage only outside the tribe. From Greek *xenos*, "stranger." Compare *xenophobe* and *xenophile*.

Xmas — legitimate abbreviation for Christmas, **X** for Greek *chi* for *Christos*.

Xylophone literally means "the voice of the wood," from the Greek *xylon* (wood) + *phone* (voice). Now the bars may be made of metal.

Yankee originates in a series of pamphlets by John Arbuthnot in 1712 in which the English were caricatured as John Bull, *Jan*, or *Janke* (**YAWN-kee**). The diminutive form was used by the Dutch colonists in North America to refer to the English. *Janke* became *Yankee*.

Zionist — The term refers to the hill on which the city of David was built. *Tslyon* means "hill" in Hebrew. The Zionist movement aiming at the establishment of a Jewish homeland in Palestine was founded by Theodor Herzl in 1896. Palestine is the land west of the Jordan, once home of the kingdoms of Israel and Judea.

Zeitgeist is German *zeit* (time) + *geist* (spirit). It means the general intellectual, moral, and cultural climate of an age.

Zounds (**zowndz**) — a mild oath meaning "God's wounds," those of Christ on the Cross.

Zucchini (**zoo-KEE-nee**) is the plural of the diminutive Italian for "gourd," *zucchino*. *Broccoli* is another vegetable name we get from Italy.

Zythepsary (**ZITH-ep-SREE**) is a brewery. It is not a word you hear every day. Neither is *zymurgy* (**ZAIM-ur-jee**) meaning "the art of brewing." *Zyme* means "fermentation." Is a brewer a *zymotechnician*? Do we imbibe *zymurgeous* beverages, cool and sparkling amber with a head of foam? If we do, we usually ask the publican (hotel keeper from *publicanus*, Latin for "tax collector") for a beer (from the Old English *beor*), an alcoholic drink made from fermented malt and flavoured with hops. Cheers!

Now let's take a closer look at some topics that were introduced earlier on in this chapter.

Bowdlerize
With a hey nonny no ...

To bowdlerize means to excise expressions felt to be indelicate. It's a form of censorship. Doctor Thomas Bowdler quit medicine when he was sixty-four, in the early 1800s, to surgically alter the works of Shakespeare (*The Family Shakespeare*, 1818) and other writers. He cut whatever he deemed *"unfit to be read by a gentleman in the company of ladies."* Before he died in 1825, Bowdler and his sister Harriet took a scalpel to a lot of material they thought unseemly.

The practice continues. In his book *Have A Word On Me*, Willard Espy records the story of two barges colliding on a rainy day. In court the Scottish judge can't understand a Cockney witness. When the Cockney is asked if he was surprised by the collision, the lawyer offers a translation, "I was completely taken aback." But what the witness actually said was, *"'Cor, you could 'ave buggered me through me oilskins!"*

You Can Say That Again!

Even without Bowdler's work certain words have evolved into respectability, hiding their origins in the mists of time and imprecision. For instance, *schism* (**SIZ-um**), used to describe splits in religious bodies, is etymologically associated with *shit*. Other words originally from names for feces include *poppycock*, *cockagee*, *cowslip*, and *oxlip*. *Poppycock* is from the Dutch *appekah*, meaning "soft dung." *Cockagee* is from the Irish for "dung of a goose." *Kak* is an almost universal sound for "excrement."

To be hoisted with one's own *petar*, or *petard*, is to run the risk of being blown up by an explosive charge used to breach a wall. But the word comes from the Latin *pedare*, "to fart." And, while on the topic of flatulence, *partridge* comes from the Greek *perdix* which means "farter." It is onomatopoeic for the whirring sound made by the partridge's wings when it is flushed from cover. *Fizzle*, too, comes from breaking wind — from the obsolete verb *fist*. Etymological study can be "a gas"!

To keep countenance is from the expression *keep continent* for "keeping bladder and bowels controlled." *Testimony* is from Latin *testis* meaning both "testicle" and "witness." *Avocado* comes from a Nahuacatl Indian word meaning "testicle." *Footling* means "foolish" and comes from the French *foutre* (originally "to copulate with").

During the Vietnam war, U.S. President Lyndon Johnson visited Australia to make a speech. He was to say, "Our soldiers who have passed through wish to be remembered to you." An aid caught the error in time. Australians often use *to pass through* to mean "to have sex with." The only surprise is that Johnson cared enough to make the correction. He was often quite blunt, even crude, in his off-hand remarks. Political correctness is the term given to finding a way to say something without giving offence. It isn't just a matter of recognizing that minorities (or women) may be offended. Different cultures have different taboos. Also, taboos change over time. Manhole covers are now *utility covers*. Chairmen are usually *chairpersons* or simply "*chairs*" these days. But perhaps we can draw the line at *fishers* for fishermen. Surely there are women on the boats as well as men, but perhaps the Broadcast News of Canadian Press was right during the salmon dispute between British Columbia and the United States from 1996 to 1998, when it called the people involved *fishermen* while the TV networks foolishly called them *fishers*!

Returning to Dr. Bowdler's efforts, we must point out that not all of his work to clean up the Bard's act was successful. Bowdler missed something in Shakespeare's *As You Like It*:

> It was a lover and his lass,
> With a hey, and a ho,
> And a hey nonny no ...

What did Bowdler think "hey nonny no" meant, anyway?!

Word Origins

SLANG

Slang: language that takes off its coat, spits on its hands and goes to work.

— Carl Sandburg.

As we've seen in the list of Word Origins, *slang* came to us from the Dutch. Slang is everyday language. We use it all the time. It is part of casual speech. It creeps into our more formal communications and sometimes acquires respectability. But the dictionary definition makes it clear that slang is coarse language below the level of written or colloquial speech. It is equated with jargon and cant. Sometimes it is "politically incorrect" by design, like the term *wife-beater* for the singlet or sleeveless undershirt worn by young people who know that the term is offensive, who are aware it is "blue collar" and that spouse assault is unacceptable.

Sometimes the dividing line between jargon and slang is blurred, but usually jargon means the language particular to a group or profession. It is designed to promote togetherness and to leave the uninformed out of the social and professional "loop." Take a look at the jargon entry elsewhere in this chapter.

Slang is simply linguistic innovation in a defined cultural context. In other words, it is a new idea, an invention, a new way of saying something about a particular activity. Examples are all the special words that came into being in the jazz world, from *gig* to *axe* to *chops* to *riff*. It's a huge, rich vocabulary which is meaningful to musicians but is almost impossible for outsiders to understand. Many jazz words and phrases, however, have found their way into other fields, such as rock and pop music, and even into non-musical activities. Slang is inventive and creative. Like jargon, it sets a group apart and loses potency when popularized. Semanticist S. I. Hayakawa has described slang as "the poetry of everyday language."

Slang is also anti-establishment. *Hip* and *cool* from the world of jazz are just two words from a black, creative milieu. The words were later pirated by other musicians, then by youth in general, and still later by novelists, and finally by the advertising industry. Advertisers try to use the language of their demographic and psychographic targets. *Cat* is another jazz term, meaning a "musician," a "sideman." (*Cat's ass*, not a jazz term, means "good.") Jazz isn't the only source of slang. New terms and new usage are created in sports and other fields.

Today, standard English is suspect. Abuse, bombast, and exaggerated rhetoric have devalued good English and good speech. These have also been abused by amateur grammarians who would object to the split infinitive. So a lot of people distrust the style and vocabulary of educated speech. Some even argue that good, educated speech is a snobbish affront to egalitarian democracy — a debate taken up elsewhere in this book.

Even slang is vulnerable to abuse and devaluation. If it is around long enough and used widely enough, it runs the risk of becoming acceptable, even in "polite" circles. As new slang enters the language, old slang becomes almost respectable. If it doesn't, it becomes obsolete, dated, and is discarded. No one wants to be out of step or so "unhip" as to use an outdated slang phrase or use it incorrectly. But sometimes old slang simply becomes part of everyday speech, a part of the always-growing-and-changing English vocabulary. To recall some slang from the Roaring Twenties set in an entirely novel context, consider the following story. When Pope John XXIII died, so the story goes, an irreverent but witty *Toronto Star* headline writer offered:

23 SKIDOO!

It didn't actually top the obit of course. But it proved that some old slang doesn't die or even fade from memory. The phrase dates from 1910.

SWEARING, CUSSING, AND PROFANITY

> *Cheese and rice!*
> Harmless swearing by a Mexican tour guide

Mark Twain felt the social ban on profane language deprived literature of a major, imaginative gift. Twain prided himself on his wide range of expletives (usually pronounced **EKS-pluh-tivz**, sometimes **ex-PLEE-tivz**). While shaving one morning, Twain cut himself and immediately composed a veritable symphony of blasphemy and scatological invention. His wife deplored the vulgarisms so, to shame him, she repeated all his phrases. Twain reacted, "You have the words, my dear, but you don't have the tune."

In some cultures swearing is profanity, sacred words are used in anger or contempt. In Napoleonic times French troops called the Iron Duke's men the *goddams*. Blasphemy is just one way to swear; the shock can also be caused by the breaking of taboos about sexuality or other bodily functions. The stronger the taboo, the more satisfying is the swearing. "Darn" is really no substitute for "damn."[2] The scatological outburst offers a broad range for venting anger or disdain. In some situations crude language may reflect social distinctions or history. In England, simple Anglo-Saxon words for body parts or sexual and bodily functions came to be unacceptable in polite society. *Merde* was in. *Shit* was out.

After William the Conqueror had crossed the Channel and made French the language of the wealthy and powerful, French words and even French pronunciations were in the ascendant. Saxon was out. With the

French came a new infusion of Romance (descended from Latin) words into the evolving English language.

Still, while it was "non-U" to use many short and snappy English words, some, like *dog, cow*, and *pig* managed to survive with some dignity. Terms relating to the social organization in the countryside also persist because William found the system useful. So we still have *wardens* and *bailiffs*, for instance.

Often, the best way to say something for impact and understanding in English is to make it short, simple, and to the point. That usually means employing an essentially Anglo-Saxon vocabulary. Sometimes, even today, people will find that way of expressing oneself crude. But it was the style of Winston Churchill in his most powerful oratory.

PUNS

A pun is a pistol let off at the ear; not a feather to tickle the intellect.
— Charles Lamb

The pun may be maligned as the lowest form of humour but it is a word game anyone can play with half an ear and a modicum of wit. Also known as a groaner, the pun — to be good — must actually be bad and prompt the listener to wince before trying to come up with an even more painful reply.

The word *pun* comes from the Italian *puntiglio* meaning "a fine point" or "quibble." It is the humorous use of a word to suggest different meanings or applications, or of words with the same or similar sounds but different meanings (homonyms).

Dr. Samuel Johnson, the lexicographer, when rebuked for calling the pun the lowest form of humour, was told he held that view because he couldn't make one. His response:

If I were punished,
For every pun I shed,
'Twould be a pun i' shed
Above my puny head.

It is even suggested there is some neurological fault in those who can't resist making puns. Puns occur in all languages, but English, with so many sound-alike words, is ideal for the play on words: "*A door is not a door when it's ajar.*"

For an example in another language, consider one from Albert Curtis Clark, an Oxford classicist and translator of Cicero. While visiting a farm with a friend they saw a bull servicing a cow. Clark commented: "*Omne animal post coitum triste....*" He then recalled that there was a firm of solicitors in London called Mann, Rogers, and Greaves.[3]

Back to English:

- East Coast fishermen, after failure of the cod stocks: *"There, but for the plaice of cod, go aye."*
- Hen to egg: *"Better laid than never."*
- Charles Dickens to Parisian bartender: *"It is the worst of times. I am without an idea for a new work. Let me have a vodka martini straight up."* Bartender: *"Olive or twist?"*
- Then there was the writer who found an idea for his first novel in the Wild West. He called it *A Tale Of Two Smitties.* He had headed west for inspiration. At one point, at a campfire at dusk, he put a sausage on his fork, held it over the fire and muttered, *"What the dickens! This is the best of times to roast a wurst on tines!"*
- Once upon a time, Ali Baba and his forty thieves went into a bit of a slump. Then, in a single week, they looted a caravan and stole the crown jewels from the sultan's palace. *"The robber band had snapped back!"* (*Crown jewels,* or often *family jewels,* is a euphemism for "male genitals.")
- Four ghosts were playing poker when there was a knock at the door: "Whoooo *is it?"* one asked. Answer: *"Rigor mortis. May I set in?"*

Farm puns:

- *"Sometimes it is a harrowing experience."*
- Or: *"Dairy farmers are my* kine *of people."*

Lost it at the movies:

- *"A drive-in theatre in August is the lust rows of summer."*

It must be something I ate (ET):

- *"Eating fungus is a morel issue."*
- *"The hot dog is frankly vulgar."*
- Münster cheese, Scots version: *"Loch Ness Münster."*
- In a good restaurant the chef is the master. The sous chef (**SOO SHEF**) is only *"parsley responsible."*
- Caviar from Ireland would be the *"Roes of Tralee."*
- Rabbit is a favourite dish in Paris. They raise them in the *"hutch back of Notre Dame"* (Hunchback of Notre Dame).

- A new Formosan beer for the North American market: *"Taiwan On."*

Song titles lend themselves to puns:

- "Poutine on the ritz."
- "Fry me a liver."
- "Veal meat again."
- "Some day my blintz will come."

Dorothy Parker had a curt way with words. Reporting on all the beauty at a Yale prom she declared, *"If all those sweet young things were laid end to end I wouldn't be at all surprised."* On another occasion, asked to use the word *horticulture* in a sentence, she said: *"You can lead a horticulture, but you can't make her think."*

In Hollywood, Bette Davis once described a starlet as *"the original good time that was had by all."*

Before putting the pun to rest for the time being, let's give James Boswell the last, tolerant word: "I think no innocent species of wit or pleasantry should be suppressed; and that a good pun may be admitted among the smaller excellencies of lively conversation."

JARGON

The most valuable of all talents is that of never using two words where one will do.

— Jefferson

Jonathan Swift observed about lawyers and lawmakers that a fog can descend when they start to speak. Lawyers are always being told — sometimes even by other lawyers, like the Law Society of Upper Canada — that they should speak and write in plain English. The idea is that the law should be readily understood by the people it is written to serve. But, all too often, the idea seems to be obfuscation so that a lawyer's interpretive services will be required. Swift put the problem this way:

It is likewise to be observed that this society of lawyers hath a peculiar cant and jargon of their own, that no other mortal can understand, and wherein all their laws are written which they take special care to multiply; whereby they have wholly confounded the very essence of truth and falsehood.

Thus, jargon is language peculiar to a group or profession. But it can also be defined as confused or meaningless talk. Here is an example:

You Can Say That Again!

Oh Parent, at present deemed to be domiciled in the
stratosphere,
May Your name be established and maintained on the highest
level of sacrosanctity,
May You be allotted and obtain an area of control with
appropriate powers of administration.
May Your policy be fully executed on a geo-political basis as
well as in the normal stratospherical sphere of influence.

Translation:

Our Father, which art in heaven,
Hallowed be Thy name,
Thy kingdom come,
Thy will be done, in earth as it is in heaven.

Nearly every group builds up a special vocabulary and manner of speaking and writing. The example above is just a form of obtuse bureaucratic jargon contrasted with the simple poetic English of the King James Bible.

As shown earlier, legalese is probably the most reviled jargon. In most fields practitioners argue their innocence, saying they use a special vocabulary to be precise, to avoid misunderstanding or ambiguity. That's the case put by lawyers. Medicine and pharmacology use Greek and Latin terms in their jargons. In the United States, the Pentagon has taken military obfuscation to new lows, but it is just an extension of age-old military circumlocution (studied indirection of speech).

Social workers and psychiatrists, bankers and brokers — even broadcasters and journalists — have jargon. There is a special language in sports. It's used by small groups of cognoscenti (knowledgeable fans) in individual sports — the languages of professional hockey, or baseball, or thoroughbred horse racing. Jargon that starts as an insider's fashionable bureaucratic vocabulary can soon sneak into other applications and into the popular vocabulary. For just a few that corrupted our discourse in the nineties, consider: *dimensionalization, holistic profit, ideation, Millennial Generation, paradigm shift, scenario-based planning, think out of the box,* and *push the envelope.*

It isn't enough to condemn jargon as grandiloquent bureaucratese. Admittedly, there is an element of that in most jargons, as in the Lord's Prayer above. But lawyers use a combination of "whereas's" and "wherefores" and "parties of the first and second part" along with their own peculiar syntax which grows like mould on old velum. Their jargon is a combination of specialized terminology and wilful affectation designed to keep the uninitiated in the dark.

We find jargon baffling in tax returns and insurance contracts. And the jargon barrier can prevent professional groups from achieving their public-relations goals. Too often members of such special groups forget how to communicate with anyone outside their group. Sometimes the problem for those receiving their message is not lack of understanding but boredom.

Rawson's *Dictionary of Euphemisms and Other Doubletalk* (1993) introduced the idea of a "fog or pomposity index." The FOP compares the length of the euphemism to the word or phrase replaced, with an extra point given for each extra letter, syllable, or word in the jargon. For example, *medicine* is eight letters, three syllables, but *medication* has ten letters and an extra syllable, thus earning eleven points for the comparison (8 into 11 for a FOP index of 1.4). *Intestinal fortitude* rather than *guts* gets a FOP index of 6.5. At the beginning of the twentieth century, newspapers aimed to simplify the language so immigrants learning English would be able to read them and benefit. The Flesch test offered a way to measure the readability of the prose, rating it by age levels. A twelve-year-old's reading ability was the target. (How much has changed?)

Examples of jargon expressing business hypocrisy are: *dehire, deselect, dislocate, excessed, surplused, transitional,* and *downsizing,* all of which deal with expedient firing and ignore the personal trauma of job loss. The emotive reality is taken out of the situation; a euphemism pretends to take a technical or clinical approach to a necessary evil. The human consequences of the acts are made secondary to "the bottom line." Of course, this means someone can escape from a social responsibility. If you don't mind being misled by fuzzy language, grab your curriculum vitae (resumé) for a *holiday career open house* for *seasonal positions.* These will be Christmas-holiday, part-time, short-term jobs at minimum wage — nothing to do with careers. Look out for the ads for *business development assistants.* These advertisers are really looking for low-cost receptionists. The same goes for the term *sales associate* when Walmart and other employers look for low-wage sales clerks. And, in real-estate ads, be sure to translate *handyman's special* into "This place will need a lot of time-consuming and costly restoration work." Governments always try to put a positive spin on their acts, such as the Canadian government changing *Unemployment Insurance* to *Employment Insurance.* And when the Chrétien government changed the Canada and Quebec Pension system and Old Age Security, they invented the term *Senior's Benefit* (higher contributions for lower payouts and a lower threshold-tax clawback)! Sometimes a euphemism is simply an insult.

We are in a war of words, or, more precisely, a war about a fog of words designed to soften or hide reality — in short, to lie. Convoluted claptrap turns up in car-rental agreements, politics, insurance policies, legal contracts, mortgages, banking documents, consumer-product warrantees, government advertising, and so on. It is the obfuscators versus the proponents of plain English. Once again, *caveat emptor!*

The Plain English Campaign in the United States, with headquarters in Miami, preaches the advantages of simplicity over pomposity. Founder Chrissie Maher used to send cow entrails to obfuscators in Britain. "Tripe for tripe," she said. Micki Oster, CEO of the U. S. campaign, provides the following examples of obnoxious jargon:

> *Involuntary conversion of a 747* — a plane crash
> *Negative patient-care outcome* — death
> *Vertically deployed anti-personnel device* — a bomb
> *Customer conveyance mobile lounge* — a bus

Chrissie Maher came to public attention when she shredded hard-to-understand British government forms in front of Parliament. When a Bobbie arrived at Westminster and read her a two-hundred-word sentence from an 1834 police act, Chrissie made her point by asking, "Does that mean we have to stop?" The media loved it. Maher was a plain-English legend. She even got to the Iron Lady, Prime Minister Margaret Thatcher. It took time to start the change, but the U.K. government reviewed more than 170,000 forms, abolished 36,000 of them, and revised 56,000.

Brevity is not just the soul of wit. It's the hallmark of strong, clear writing. It makes sense to say it with economy and simplicity. If the goal is to be readily understood, there is no point in adding words, using multisyllabic words or words that only specialists can comprehend. The best guide to effective editing is *The Elements of Style,* the little paperback style guide by Strunk and White which has been reprinted many times. It argues against jargon, against unnecessary words, against affectation and for simplicity. It makes a powerful argument for short, strong words. It echoes Julius Caesar's statement that "an unusual word should be shunned as a ship should shun a reef."

A String of Euphemisms
"What the Sam Hill!" instead of "What the Hell!"

Patrick "Paddy" James Nolan departed Ireland in 1889. He practiced law in Calgary, Alberta, until his death in 1913. At one point in his career he had to inform a father that his son had been executed. The deceased was a remittance man. His father was an English baronet. Nolan remembered an obituary story written by his friend Bob Edwards of the *Calgary Eye-opener* about the hanging of a man named Clancy at Fort Saskatchewan. So Nolan wrote his letter as follows:

"My Lord,

I regret that I have to inform you that your son met his death last Friday morning whilst taking part as a principal in an important public ceremony. Unhappily, the platform on which he was standing gave way.

I have the honour to remain, Sir,

Your Most Obedient Servant,
Patrick James Nolan,
Barrister-at-Law."

When there was still a Fleet Street of newspapers in London, their journalists would describe a member of Parliament as a "swordsman" or a "fighter pilot." These terms were widely understood to mean that the individual was, to use another euphemism, a "ladies' man." In other words, the M.P. was known to be "a man of affairs." These days the tabloids in the United Kingdom and in North America are less likely to use euphemisms. They might use the term *family jewels* to mean "genitals." And they are more likely to headline their stories of indiscretions with clarion banners like:

SEX-DRIVEN SENATOR RESIGNS
or
SEXAGENARIAN SEXPOT QUITS LORDS

U.S. President Bill Clinton faced direct accusations of indiscretions while he was governor of Arkansas and while in the White House, and the newspapers, including the *Washington Post* as well as other reputable journals, spelled out the charges in minute detail. The suggestion of peculiar private parts made it into news columns everywhere and headlined supermarket tabloids. So things have changed from the days when this headline hid a message:

MINISTER APPEARS FATIGUED

If an indiscretion doesn't compromise the office and if the disclosure of the act will only hurt an individual and his or her family, why bother disclosing it? Is the story just amusing gossip or does the character flaw jeopardize the public interest? Some circumlocutions are clearly deceitful, designed to hide something or to misinform. Watch for them in advertising promises to protect the environment or public health — or in military prose. *Defence* departments were once *war* departments.

A Canadian politician in the House, provincial legislature, or municipal council might be described as "tired when he rose to speak in the house today." It is generally understood that in this context *tired* meant the politician was "in his cups," "merry," or "somewhat the worse for drink." Perhaps the M.P. spent too much time over cognac in the parliamentary dining room.

In ancient Greece, anyone who overindulged (drank too much of the usually watered wine) at a *symposium* was said to be *wet*, or *dipped*, or *chest protected*.

Other substitutes for *snackered* or *drunk* are: *mellow, happy, merry, pixilated, tipsy, in a fog, inebriated, intoxicated, fuddled, feeling no pain, under the influence, ripped, waxed, blotto, legless, embalmed, paralytic, pissed, pie-eyed, high as a kite,* and *pickled*. Add to the list: *fried, boiled,* and *falling down drunk*. In the 1960s, a member of the Canadian House of Commons who was sometimes described as "tired" would occasionally hold impromptu news conferences in his office while clearly in his cups. Once, he stood with his back to the door talking over his shoulder as he relieved himself into an office sink while reporters gathered at the door to hear his heavily accented and slurred words of wisdom on national affairs. He'd had a snootful. He was *ivre mort*, as the French say.

Unwell is another euphemism for inebriation, as in the play *Jeffrey Barnard Is Unwell*, a piece about a *London Spectator* writer whose column was sometimes missing because the author was "indisposed."

Now, if you ever read the following kind of newspaper story about a cabinet minister, you will know what it means:

CABINET MINISTER STOPPED BY POLICE

> ... when stopped by police,
> the minister appeared tired
> and emotional. Charges are
> pending according to police
> sources. The minister ...

Horsin' Around

Sometimes the vocabulary of a vocation or a technological sphere becomes jargon or slang; at other times it is stretched for more popular application. Think of computer terms. Or, for instance, the term *horse's ass* which refers to somebody making a fool of himself. Also from the horsey set come terms like *horse power*, applied to engines: "How many horses have you got under the hood?" "Never look a gift horse in the mouth," meaning one shouldn't question a gift by checking the nag's teeth to determine age or health. Someone has the *bit in his teeth* or is *in the saddle* when acting with determination and enthusiasm on a project or having *taken the reins* of leadership. When people act without consideration for others, we accuse them of *running roughshod*. And there's the saying, once applied to someone about to lose control, "Hold 'er Newt! She's headed for the barn!" We say the coach has a *tight rein on his players*. We say a person excited or agitated about something is *lathered*. Which is akin to what we say when someone has worked to exhaustion and been *ridden hard and put away wet*. If you are annoyed you *have a burr under your saddle*. Someone is *cavalier* when haughty, but the term once meant a "gallant or fashionable man escorting a woman." The word comes from Italian *cavallo* derived from the Latin *caballus*. *Cavalry* comes from the same source. A *gay caballero* (**KAB-al-YER-o**) is not a homosexual cowboy but a Spanish gentleman. A *cavalier* (a horseman) was a supporter of Charles I in England's Civil War.

LIMERICKS

Some samples of limericks were promised. A limerick is a humorous five-line verse. The first and second lines rhyme with the fifth. The third and fourth lines also rhyme.

"Will you come up to Limerick?" is an invitation to offer another limerick, more ribald (**RIB-uld**) than the first. Limerick is a county in North Munster in the Southwest of Ireland.

> *There was an old man of Cape Horn,*
> *Who wished he had never been born,*
> *So he sat on a chair,*
> *Till he died of despair,*
> *That dolorous old man of Cape Horn. (DAWL-ir-us)*
> — Edward Lear

> *There was a young lady of Madras,*
> *Who played croquet on the grass;*
> *She swung with great might,*
> *To her lover's delight,*
> . . . .

A PUZZLE

George Bernard Shaw was once asked by the military theorist and historian B. H. Liddell-Hart, "Do you know that *sumac* and *sugar* are the only two words in the English language that begin with *su* and are pronounced "**shu**"? Shaw replied, "Sure."

A RIDDLE?

A riddle goes, "*Angry* and *hungry* are two words ending in -*gry*. There are three words in the English language ending that way. What is the third word? Everyone knows what it means and uses it every day. Look closely, for you have already been given the third word. What is it?"

An incorrect reading of the riddle or a misunderstanding of it can lead to a list of words:

aggry — glass bead found buried in the earth in Ghana and England
anhungry — hungry
puggry — scarf worn around a hat (Hindi?)
begry — obsolete form of *beggary*
conyngry — rabbit warren (obsolete)
higrypigry — medicine used up to the 1700s to induce vomiting
kingry — child's ball game in which the winner is declared king
meagry — having a meagre appearance (obsolete)
nangry — poetic form of angry
podagry — gout (foot + ...)
skugry — scuggery, meaning concealment (obsolete)

The Answer is "language," because the first sentence is a ruse to mislead you. The key sentences are the second and third. "There are three words in 'the English language.'" What is the third word in the phrase "the English language"? Let's hope Internet bores and pedantic word worriers will let this pointless question rest. It isn't even an entertaining riddle, but it's included here because it has had a new lease on life on the Internet. There is nothing instructive about it.

VOWELS MISSING

There are some words without vowels but they aren't very useful. A *crwth* is an ancient stringed instrument. A *cwm* is a step-walled mountain basin shaped like half a bowl. A *brwk* is a brook, while a *bwrch* is a burgh or town. A *hws* is a house of course and a *pwl* is a pool. *Swrd*, you guessed it, is a sword. And *trsw* once spelled *true*, while *wp* spelled *up*. If you *wss* (use) any of these words in a written sentence you may send your reader to the library with a headache. We may have problems with English spellings today, but for the most part they make more sense now than when words that consisted of consonants were current. Thanks to the Greeks for adding vowels to the Phoenician alphabet.

James Thurber is credited with asking the muse, "What seven-letter word has three *u*'s in it?" The muse is said to have thought and then said, "I don't know, but it must be unusual."

– 30 –

The – 30 – found at the bottom of a page now simply means "The

End," but at the end of news copy it also means there will be no *adds* or *folos* on the story. What you have in hand is the final edit. There will be no rewrites.

Apocryphal or not, it is said that a surly editor at the *Cleveland Plain Dealer* used a heavy lead pencil to scrawl:

$$-\,30\,-$$

across any copy submitted. His intention, so the story goes, was to let reporters and editors know their copy could benefit by cutting thirty words. The editor insisted on tight copy. Writers and reporters soon caught on. They started typing – 30 – at the bottom of their copy to indicate the cut had already been made.

Another tale about – 30 – at the end of a story relates that it began as a telegrapher's slang expression with *30* meaning "GN" or "Goodnight, we are closing up and going home." In Morse code, numbers stood for words and sentences. The number 73 meant "kind regards." The number 88 signified "love and kisses." Railway telegraphers used a number code as well:

1	Wait a minute.
2	Very important.
3	What is the time?
4	From which point shall I repeat?
77	I have a message for you.

Yet another story is told about the origin of – 30 – ; it suggests that the symbol comes from typesetting. The maximum line or length of slug on Linotype hot-lead casting machines was thirty picas, or five inches. When an operator reached thirty picas, the limit had been reached. End of story.

$$-\,30\,-$$

Notes

1. Cannabis, pot, marijuana, Mary Jane.

2. Hollywood's Hays office made Clark Gable in *Gone With The Wind* change the emphasis in the sentence: "Frankly, Scarlett, I don't GIVE a damn!" They said, if he was to say the word *damn,* he'd have to put the emphasis elsewhere in the sentence — on *give*!

3. "All animals are sad after intercourse," is the translation. The lawyers' names mean, "Mankind fornicates and grieves."

You Can Say That Again!

Quiz 4
?

1) The Spanish word *cojones* refers to _____
   Write *cojones* phonetically. _____

2) Define **spoonerism** and give an example. _____

3) The word *algebra* comes from which language? _____

4) *Bible*, the word, comes from which ancient Phoenician city?

5) *Fan* comes from which Latin word for an overwrought religious person? _____

6) Give an example of an **eponym**. _____

7) *Riding*, for an electoral district, comes from an old English word, an arithmetic term. What was the word? _____

8) *Umbra* means _____

9) In a word, what is *negative patient care outcome*? _____

10) The **FOP Index** deals with what problem in writing and speech?

11) In a telegrapher's number code, what did *30* mean? _____

12) *Thug* originated in which language? _____

13) Which language gave us *Yankee*? _____

14) *Petard*, which means in English "a small bomb" or "a firework," comes to us from Latin *pedere* via French *pétard*. The original meaning referred to what embarrassing problem? _____

For answers, see Appendix A.

CHAPTER FOUR

English:
from Sanskrit to Chaucer

Chapter Four

English:
from Sanskrit to Chaucer

The day the gates go up, that day it begins to die.
— H. L. Mencken
(commenting on the living language)

Change is inevitable in language. Usage changes over time, as do spelling and pronunciation.

In the fourteenth century, when English was in a turmoil of diverse influences including French and Latin, Chaucer wrote of the "*gret diversite in English and in writyng of oure tonge.*"

William Caxton, England's first printer, offered an example of this lack of uniformity in 1490. He wrote about some merchants headed for Holland but becalmed in the Thames.

They needed food and drink, so they went ashore. One of them "*cam in-to an hows and axed for mete; and specyally he axed after eggys. And the good wyf answerde that she coude not speke no Frenshe.*"

The merchant was annoyed because he thought he had been speaking good English. But a friend with a wider vocabulary helped out by telling the woman they were looking for "eyren." We presume they got their eggs.

Caxton asked, "*Loo, what sholde a man in thyse dayes wryte, egges or eyren. Certaynly it is harde to playse eueryman by cause of dyuersite and chaunge of langage.*"

Eventually we settled on the Scandinavian word *egg.* But in Caxton's language you can certainly see the variety of spelling. You wonder about the various pronunciations. And you can see the French influence in the word-ending *e* and in words like *langage*, pronounced in French **lawn-GAHZH.**

This chapter traces the history of the English language and takes a look at the many English words that come from other languages. One source of frustration for people trying to learn English is its inconsistency. Its spelling doesn't necessarily point you to the correct pronunciation. While phonics help children learn to read, English can be misleading. *Often* is **AWF-'n,** *vegetable* is said **VEJ-tuh-bul** and *slough* is **SLOO.** *Slow* sounds like *flow, blow* sounds like *no,* but *now* sounds like *cow.*

Our brief history of English ends with some samples of the tricks the language can play on us just when we think we understand it.

Back in the Neolithic age, about 3000 B.C., the Indo-Europeans were living in either eastern or north-central Europe. Some of the language differentiation began with migrations into India, Greece, and western Europe. The earliest documents in Sanskrit and Greek date from between 3000 and 500 B.C. From 500 B.C. to 300 A.D., the Germanic tribes and the Celts had contact with the Romans. The Gothic Bible was created around 350 A.D. Patterns set by the Greeks and Romans permeate our civilization. Half our vocabulary comes from the so-called dead languages — words and concepts like politics, science, art, music, religion, athletics, and philosophy. *Barbaros* is what Greeks called anyone who didn't speak Greek in the Hellenic world of the ninth century B.C. (see **barbarous**, Chapter 3). The Greek culture had a broad reach over time and geography. For example, they named Naples (*Neapolis*), meaning "new city."

By 500 A.D., Anglo-Saxon invasions led to the emergence of Old English. The English names for almost all domestic animals come from that time: *cat, dog, horse, hound, sow, pig, sheep, cow, ox, duck, hen,* and *chick*. The first appearance of *dog* turned up in a translation of the Latin *canis* in 1050 as *docgena*. About two hundred years later it turned up again as *dogge*. *Hound* was the common word for the animal until the sixteenth century.

Between 700 and 1000 A.D., there were Danish and Norse raids. The Viking raids left their marks but the West Saxon dialect was the main language in England. Old French and other Romance languages were developing.

The Norman Conquest (1066) led to the replacement of the ruling class in England by French speakers.[1] At this time nearly all the names of wild animals entered the language: *lion, tiger, elephant, bear,* and *wolf*. Before this period there had been much borrowing from Norse. Between 1300 and 1475 the emergence of English (the East Midland dialect as it was spoken in London) coincided with the literary production of Chaucer, Wyclif, and the mystery and morality plays.

> *"Be there proclamacioin, that sure they be, that willen toward our liege lord the kyng, beying atte harfleure, in the costes of Normandye, that god him spede with corne, brede, mele, or flour, wynde...."*

That's part of a proclamation issued to assemble supplies for King Henry V who was invading France in 1415. The complete proclamation illustrates just how much the language has changed. At that time there was no standardized spelling. As mentioned above, there were lots of *e*'s on the ends of words and many influences from French. A hundred years earlier French had been even more dominant. The English of that time is almost totally unfamiliar and indecipherable for most of us today. Of course, with the Norman invasion, French had become the official language of Britain.

It is appropriate to point out that class and social distinctions influence our views, even our value systems, let alone our language. Anglo-Saxon words were considered lower class by the Normans who took over England. The prejudice continued for generations. It is with us today in the view that certain short Anglo-Saxon words are unacceptable in polite company. Certainly we can say "cow," "pig," and "dog," but when it comes to defecation we had better say "*merde.*"

In summary, here are some of the important events and developments in the history of English:

3000 to 500 B.C. — Indo-European languages including Germanic. Early documents written in Greek and Sanskrit.

500 to I B.C. — Celts in Britain. The Roman Empire's first contacts with German tribes. Latin's influence starts to spread.

1 to 300 A.D. — The Romanization of Britain. The migrations of German tribes.

300 to 500 —Anglo-Saxon invasions. Beginning of Old English. The Gothic Bible.

500 to 700 — Adoption of the alphabet.

700 to 1000 — Norse raids. West Saxon dialect. More Latin borrowings.

1000 to 1150 — Viking raids. Norman Conquest. Borrowings from Norse. French becomes the official tongue.

1300 to 1475 — Chaucer, Wyclif. Emergence of English, a London dialect. The Middle English period.

1475 to 1650 — Caxton and printing. Revival of the study of Latin and Greek. Shakespeare and Milton. Loss of the final *e.* Beginning of the standardization of spelling.

1650 to 1800 — Attempts at conformity of English usage, pronunciation, and spelling. English spreads around the world and borrows widely.

1800 — Rapid change under the influence of science, technology, education, literacy, dictionaries, radio, television, and the computer.[2]

THE LANGUAGE OF SHAKESPEARE

The printer Caxton (1422-1491) had a problem Shakespeare didn't have. Caxton had to choose from various dialects. He chose the ones most commonly heard in London. He printed his first English text in 1474 and produced, among other works, editions of *Le Morte d'Arthur* and Chaucer's *Canterbury Tales*. Caxton himself was advised at one point that his polished and ornate diction *"could not be understande of comyn people."*

The pamphleteer Thomas Nash wrote words full of praise in 1592 about the poets of the time of Good Queen Bess who had, *"made the vulgar sort here in London ... to aspire to a richer puritie of speach, than is communicated with the Cominalitie of any nation under heaven."*

As Ben Jonson (1572–1637), Christopher Marlowe (1564–93), and William Shakespeare (1564–1616) created their works of genius in the new language, a major infusion of Latin continued. Less than fifty years before the Bard was born Sir Thomas More wrote his *Utopia* in Latin. Latin was the Esperanto of More's time. Bacon's *Novum Organum* was also written in Latin (1620).

As the language of London was developing and becoming the standard for English, foreigners regarded the tongue as "the scum of many languages." It was a time of invention of words, of alteration and adaptation. In Elizabethan grammar almost any part of speech could be used as another. Shakespeare's English was one of great vitality. Poetry and flights of rhetoric were part of its charm. The prime quality of Elizabethan English was its passion for free experiment, its willingness to use every form of verbal wealth, to try anything.

The dramatists and poets brought to it not just the language understood by Londoners, but a lot of foreign input as well. Among other works, Marlowe wrote *Doctor Faustus,* while Jonson created *Volpone* and *Bartholomew Fair.*

By Shakespeare's time the English of London was considered the best spoken form and was established as the language of literature. It was, *"the usual speach of the Court and that of London and the shires lying about."*

Phonologists are unable to completely capture the true sounds of Elizabethan English. Often what was a good rhyme then no longer works for us. Falstaff pronounced *reasons* as *raisins*. So there was fun in *"If reasons were as plentie as Black-berries..."* English is still changing of course. It changes in pronunciation, spelling and punctuation, accidence and syntax; words fall into disuse or change their meanings. *Accidence*, by the way, is the part of grammar that deals with the variable parts or inflections of words.

In Shakespeare's time words were given different meanings as it suited. Context determined their sense. *Bombast* originally meant "cotton wool" or "stuffing." *Baste* came to apply to both sewing and cooking. For another example, *confederate* was a common verb in Tudor times. Shakespeare loved puns, but as vocabulary has changed over the years our understanding of his wit has withered. Now footnotes are necessary to explain Shakespeare's puns, and a pun looses its point if it has to be explained.

Malvolio would *baffle* Sir Toby but has to bear Olivia's pity: "*Alas poore Foole, how have they baffl'd thee....*"

Change and adaptability are characteristic of English. Certain words used just a few decades ago are now obsolete. Words that meant one thing a decade ago mean something very different today. Consider the word *gay*. Consider the word *bop*. Grammar and pronunciation change too, sometimes so slowly we don't even notice. Schedule is pronounced **SKED-jul** in the United States. It's **SHED-jul** in Britain. It can be either way in Canada. The **SHED-jul** pronunciation came from French influence. The word ending *-our* is still common in Canada, but the American *-or* spreads and the debate goes on. English continues to evolve. It is alive and adaptable, always in flux. That is one of its greatest strengths.

While it adopts words from many cultures, English has invaded numerous other languages. The French had to decide if *microchip* was masculine or feminine, *le* or *la, un* or *une.* The Russians have adopted *komputers* and *miksers* and *tosters* for use in their homes and in their conversation. In Japan a gin and tonic is a *jintonikku* and ice cream is *aisukierimu.* Among the flavours of *yoguraeto* are *chokoreto, banira,* and *sutoroberi.*

AARDVARK TO ZEBRA — AFRIKAANS TO BANTU

Language is an inventory of human experience.
— L. W. Lockhart

English is a voracious language. It devours words as it needs them. If a word in another language conveys a unique meaning, then English makes it its own. *Aardvark, bazaar, ukelele, teepee,* and *zebra* are words that make that point. Can you link them with their languages of origin?

aardvark	Afrikaans
moose	Algonkian
alcohol	Arabic

You Can Say That Again!

Now I surely will not plague you
With such words as vague and ague,
But be careful how you speak,
Say – break, steak, but bleak and streak,
Previous, precious, fuchsia, via,
Pipe, snipe, recipe and choir,
Cloven, oven, how and low,
Script, receipt, shoe, poem, toe,
Hear me say devoid of trickery
Daughter, laughter and Terpsichore,
Typhoid, measles, topsails, aisles,
Exiles, similes, reviles,
Wholly, holly, signal, signing,
Thames, examining, combining;
Scholar, vicar and cigar,
Solar, mica, war and far,
From desire: desirable — admirable from admire,
Clatham, brougham, renown but known,
Knowledge, done but gone and tone, one,
Anemone, Balmoral,
Kitchen, lichen, laundry, laurel,
Gertrude, German, wind and mind,
Scene, Melpomene, mankind,
Tortoise, turquoise, chamois, leather,
Reading, Reading, heathen, heather,
This phonetic labyrinth,
Gives moss, gross, brook, brooch, ninth, plinth,
Billet does not end like ballet,
Bouquet, wallet, mallet, chalet,
Blood and flood are not like food,
Nor is mould like should and would.
Banquet is not nearly parquet,
Which is said to rhyme with "darky."
Viscous, viscount, load and broad,
Toward, to forward, to reward.
And your pronunciation is o.k.
When you say correctly croquet,
Rounded, wounded, grieve and sieve,
Friend and fiend, alive and live,
Liberty, library, heave and heaven,
Rachel, ache, moustache, eleven,
We say hallowed, but allowed,
People, leopard, towed but vowed,
Make the difference, moreover,